Disciplining Your Child

VICKI PORETTA
& ERICKA LUTZ

**alpha
books**

A Division of Macmillan General Reference
A Simon & Schuster Macmillan Company
1633 Broadway, New York, NY 10019-6785

Macmillan Publishing books may be purchased for business or sales promotional use. For information please write: Special Markets Department, Macmillan Publishing USA, 1633 Broadway, New York, NY 10019-6785.

International Standard Book Number: 0-02-861950-1
Library of Congress Catalog Card Number: 97-073175
99 98 97   8 7 6 5 4 3 2

Interpretation of the printing code: the rightmost number of the first series of numbers is the year of the book's printing; the rightmost number of the second series of numbers is the number of the book's printing. For example, a printing code of 97-1 shows that the first printing occurred in 1997.

Printed in the United States of America

Alpha Development Team

Brand Manager: Kathy Nebenhaus
Executive Editor: Gary M. Krebs
Managing Editor: Bob Shuman
Senior Editor: Nancy Mikhail
Development Editor: Jennifer Perillo
Editorial Assistant: Maureen Horn
Director of Editorial Services: Brian Phair
Development Editor: Kate Layzer
Production Editor: Laura Uebelhor
Copy Editor: Laura Uebelhor
Illustrator: George McKeon
Designer: George McKeon
Indexer: Joe Long
Production Team: Tricia Flodder, Mary Hunt, Pamela Woolf

Look for these additional titles in the Mom's Guides™ series...

Check out the Mom's Guide Web site!!!
www.momsguide.com

Contents

Introduction

Hey, Mom! Yeah, you with the beeper in your pocket, the defrosting chicken on the kitchen counter, and the car pool schedule tattooed on your forearm! Remember back when the kids were babies and it was all about diaper rash and chicken pox? I see your eyes growing misty—you remember those days fondly. Yikes! Your kids are bigger now and, as they careen toward adolescence, discipline is becoming more and more challenging. Here's the million-dollar question: How do you raise a responsible child without becoming a tyrant? What works?

This is a book about Discipline-with-a-capital-D. Hey, put away the bullwhip, Sally! No, don't reach for your belt, and please, take off that black leather corset. This is a family book, and that's not what I have in mind. I'm talking about disciplining your children. Being a parent can be utterly frustrating. Do you ever find yourself raging, yelling, hitting, or seething? Do you ever wonder how your beautiful little baby turned into this insubordinate monster in front of you? Then this book is for you.

Mom's Motto #42: Nothing is easy with kids, and nothing is ever going to be. Yet nobody said it couldn't be easier. I can help. The *Mom's Guide to Disciplining Your Child* gives you an approach to discipline for kids from middle childhood through early adolescence (ages 8 through 14), an approach based on mutual respect, communication, and effective tactics that will make life easier for yourself and for your kids.

Being a parent matters. All moms want to be good parents, and yet nobody is perfect (not even Mom). So much is at stake. All parents want and need, their kids to turn out okay. Maybe you picked up this book because you're curious. Maybe you picked it up because you're feeling guilty. Maybe (egad!) somebody bought it for you. I know a mom—balancing a family and a job—who regularly dissolves in tears after family squabbles, crying, "I was a great mom of one child, but now that I have three I'm awful."

Cool it with the guilt, don't panic, and give yourself a break. It's your kid's job to know all your buttons and push them. Challenging the world is part of being a human being. And it's your job to learn how to be the best parent you can be—to provide safe limits, love, respect, and gentle correction. The *Mom's Guide to Disciplining Your Child* can help you teach discipline now and save you from agony later. If you're feeling out of control, this book can also help you get back on track. Look, you're not ever going to be the "Perfect Parent." You can be a better one.

Like you, we are moms-in-the-trenches. Like all parents, we have parenting concerns, especially around the tricky area of discipline. Luckily for you, we have a passion for research. We've read about discipline, we've thought about discipline, we've lived discipline, and you get to reap the fruits of our labor. This book combines our mom's voice of experience and insight with information compiled from experts galore in one easy-to-carry volume.

EXTRAS

Along with the main text of this book, you'll find some other features: tips, advice, information, and warnings. No need to delve too deeply for these juicy nuggets; they're all in bite-sized chunks that can be easily identified by the following icons:

WISE WORDS

Here are words to help you build your "disciplinary" vocabulary. You'll also find them collected at the back of the book in the glossary.

MOM ALWAYS SAID

Warning! You're stepping into a danger zone! These features will alert you to potential danger areas—in parenting, in discipline, in society, in life. Pay attention to Mom, now.

MOM KNOWS BEST

Here's wise advice for you, ideas to ponder, and nuggets of wisdom. Listen up!

ALL IN THE FAMILY

This feature gives you facts and figures, not-so-trivial trivia, and tidbits of wisdom about family matters, parenting, and discipline.

A NOTE ON PRONOUNS

Throughout the *Mom's Guide to Disciplining Your Child*, I've alternated gender pronouns and examples. Except in some very specific circumstances (and you'll know what I'm talking about when you get there), the examples and pronouns used are random and may be applied to kids of either sex.

SPECIAL THANKS FROM THE PUBLISHER TO THE TECHNICAL REVIEWER

The *Mom's Guide to Disciplining Your Child* was reviewed by an expert in the field who checked for technical accuracy and provided a wealth of experience, valuable suggestions, and thoughtful insights about the contents.

Our special thanks are extended to Margaret M. Edwards, Ph.D. Dr. Edwards has over 20 years of experience in child psychology, counseling, and parent education in the San Francisco Bay area. She earned her Ph.D. at the Wright Institute in Berkeley. Since 1979, she has worked for Kaiser Permenente as an individual and multi-family counselor and parent educator, and she is currently a staff psychologist and the Director of Training for the Department of Psychiatry. Dr. Edwards has a private psychiatric practice in San Francisco focusing on psychotherapy with adolescents and young adults. She is a mother and a grandmother.

Acknowledgments

Vicki Poretta wishes to acknowledge her husband, Joe, and their two children for their inspiration in the creation of the *Mom's Guide* series. Vicki also wishes to acknowledge John Rourke, Joe Fallon, and Henry Poydar of Big World Media, Inc., for their creative development and marketing of related *Mom's Guide* publications and products. She would also like to thank her friends at Poretta and Orr, Inc., especially Peter Laughton, for their creative help. Vicki also wishes to thank her many "sports mom" friends who lent their support and ideas along the cheering sidelines of their kids' games.

Ericka Lutz wants to express her greatest thanks to many individuals for their information, hard work, and loving support while this book was being written. Annie McManus shared her skilled insights, wise approaches, and resource recommendations. The Elder Moms in her life, especially Karla Lutz (her own mom) and Peggy Roche (her pal Tilly's mom), gave wisdom, guidance, and support. Her agent Andree Abecassis was always enthusiastic and supportive—a one-woman cheerleading squad (*sans* pom-poms). Nancy Mikhail, Jennifer Perillo, Kate Layzer, and Laura Uebelhor provided keen editorial guidance.

On the home front, Ericka's extended family of family and friends kept her planted, sunned, and well-watered. Her partner-in-life, Bill Sonnenschein, shouldered far more than his usual equal share of child care and household duty and did it in his usual passionate and loving style. Aaron and Rachel Sonnenschein reminded her with their terrific beings that it's all worth it. Her daughter Annie provided love and well-needed distraction. Of special note among her magnificent group of friends: Tilly provided solitude, friendship, and beach access. Ailsa provided coffee dates—until she stopped drinking coffee—and the Big Ear when she got distracted. Thanks, everybody, for helping her serenitize her multitasking.

The Gentle Disciplinarian

Here's the first thing you should know about, Mom: I'm a skeptic. When I pick up a book—especially an advice book—the first thing I want to know is: "Where's the author coming from? What's her perspective?"

I'm going to assume you're like me and that you want to know about my approach and my perspectives, so let's get that out of the way first. In this chapter, I'm going to define and clarify just what I mean by discipline and talk a little about my general parenting philosophy. I know you want specifics—tools, tips, and tricks. Don't worry, we'll cover all that—and more—in later chapters.

MOM KNOWS BEST

A parent's attitude about discipline is part of her entire parenting approach. Discipline is part of everyday life with your kids.

WHAT DO YOU MEAN, "DISCIPLINE," MOM?

Discipline is a big, scary word. Let's get one thing straight right at the beginning of the book: Discipline and punishment are not the same thing!

I used to hate the word "discipline"—many people do. The problem was that I'd confused discipline with punishment. When I looked up the word "discipline" in the dictionary, I was surprised at the word's positive implications. Discipline comes from the word "disciple," meaning "a pupil," and the definition of discipline includes words such as "instruction," "teaching," "learning," and "to train or develop."

In her book *Parent Awareness Training*, Saf Lerman calls discipline "a process whereby children learn to make parental standards their own. It is a slow gradual process that extends throughout childhood. The goal of discipline is the creation of a strong and reliable conscience in a child."

I don't know about you, but I can live with these definitions. Discipline is about learning values. How do kids learn? How do they learn the kinds of behavior that will make them cool, kind adults who can really make a contribution to the world? Kids learn through guidance—but not the kind of guidance that makes them feel like scum at the bottom of the barrel. They learn through experience; they learn when they feel good about learning, and not before. Discipline teaches a way to *be* in the world.

Punishment? Gross!

The words "discipline" and "punishment" are often used interchangeably. I looked up the word "punishment" in the dictionary.

Yuck. That definition uses words such as "suffering," "pain," "loss," and "retribution." As a modern mom, I shudder at these kinds of words.

Punishment is too often connected with a loss of sense of control of the parent. The parent wants to "teach him a lesson." Well, you can't teach somebody a lesson unless he wants to be taught, and punishing him is not going to make him more receptive. Punishment, even when done with the best intentions, will lower your child's self-respect, and fostering self-respect is vital to raising a responsible, loving person. I'm not going to use the word "punishment"—or the concept—in this book.

> **MOM ALWAYS SAID**
>
> Watch out when you find yourself thinking that you want to "improve" your child—this urge is usually connected with disappointment and judgment about who your child is. Work instead toward specific goals: better grades, smoother relationships, and so on.

So It All Comes Down To...

Enough of other people's definitions, I know you're wondering what I mean by discipline. Discipline isn't just a word or a definition. In my book (hey, this is my book!), discipline is an approach to life. So in a nutshell, here's my general approach to discipline:

- ◆ Respect your children and yourself.

- ◆ Encourage and reward reasonable and responsible behavior.

- ◆ Prevent problems through understanding, communication, and modeling.

- ◆ Set clear, reasonable standards and limits.

- ◆ Understand the problem—what's behind the behavior?

- ◆ Provide related, respectful, and reasonable responses to all behaviors.

Discipline is the process of instilling values in your child through example, encouragement, and gentle guidance.

THE ART OF PAYING ATTENTION

As the mom of an older kid or kids, you're probably very involved in activities other than parenting. That's as it should be. It's the millennium, and all moms, whether they work out of the home or as a homemaker (or both), are busy. But parenting requires time, and effective, positive discipline requires paying attention to your child, and that means really focusing on what's going on in your child's life.

Here's the usual story: When your baby is a baby, you read all the books. You call your pediatrician when your baby gets a pimple, convinced the little morsel is dying. You stare into the crib for hours, willing Junior to *breathe.* Slowly, as Baby (much to your surprise) continues to inhale and exhale on his own, you relax. Time flies by and you get through early childhood. Now in the middle and later years of childhood, your kids are reaching out to the world and becoming more and more independent, and parenting is (phew!) far less intensive than those early years of it's-been-20-minutes-between-diaper-changes.

All this is normal. Yes, you can and should have a life.

Yet, here's the odd thing: Just as you're feeling the cool winds of freedom, just as Sweet Baboo seems to need you no more, that's *exactly* when she needs your attention more than ever! Not the intensive, hands-on, every-minute attention of parenting an infant or small child, but a different quality—a serious, respectful, consistent look at what's actually going on inside her mind, in her school, with her friends, with her life.

It's time to focus, again, on the art of paying attention.

ALL IN THE FAMILY

Parenting is never over, nor is worrying about your kids. I have a dear pal whose kids are long gone from the nest—the boy is 26, the girl is 23—but he worries about them like they were still babies. Of course, in a way they are, they're baby adults, and baby *anythings* are always vulnerable.

Zen Master Mama

Paying attention is not just about being physically present—it means learning how to listen to your kids, how to talk to them, and how to respond to their actions. The art of paying attention to your kids is a lot like the focus required for many of the martial arts—karate, tae kwon do, tai chi, and so on—and most of the Eastern meditations. One of the main tenets of all these studies is the importance of paying attention.

The Discipline of Discipline

Here's another parallel: In the study of martial arts, the word "discipline" is often used. Meditation is also considered a "discipline." Just for a moment, let's think of this child discipline thing as a martial art, or as a study in meditation. Just as it takes a lot of practice to become a black belt in karate or a Zen master, so it takes time and practice to gain confidence and aptitude in disciplining your children.

Discipline begins from the outside—taught by you—and moves to the inside as your kid develops his conscience and sense of responsibility. Discipline is crucial if your child is to develop the capacity to respect himself and others and to be a responsible, compassionate person. You and your child are entering into this study together.

For some it comes naturally, but most of us need to practice—to be disciplined about learning the discipline of discipline. You can pay attention anywhere. Even in your busy, distracted life, you can take a moment here and there to do a little "meditation" on how your kid is behaving—and what your response should be. (I know, it's hard to think of it as "a meditation" when you're cruising down the highway, late, on your way to soccer practice with two screaming kids in the back and an ache in your right arm where your carpal tunnel syndrome is acting up because you've been working at the computer for too many long hours.)

I'm not asking for *more* time—life is stressed as it is. I'm reminding you of what matters—the quality of life. Paying attention and applying reasonable, appropriate discipline will improve the quality of life—and there's always time for quality.

I LOVE YOU, GOTTA RUN...

Wow, this is the hard part. How do you stay involved, focus, pay attention, get the report written, the dry cleaning picked up, the dog washed and the deal signed, and still manage to let your little birds learn to fly?

Let's stick for a minute to the martial arts and meditation metaphor. All these studies talk about the search for balance in life, in our bodies, in our minds. Yowza. Is this applicable to parenting, or what? Parenting is a balancing act. You'll spend all your years as a parent walking the fine line between involvement and letting go. Somehow, you've gotta do both at the same time!

Mom's Motto #12: You have influence, but not control.

You know it as well as I do—you're not the only thing that matters in your children's lives. The older they get, the less they want to listen to poor old you.

Yet, no matter how the little creeps try to deny it, you do matter. Remember in the movie *Star Wars* how Obi Wan Kenobi's voice resounded in Luke's ears during the crisis points ("The Force, Luke, trust the Force")? Your voice of "wisdom" will echo in your kid's ears forever, long after you're gone. How do you want that voice to sound? "Johnny, you bad boy, stop that this instant!" Or—in a gentle, melodious tone, of course—"That isn't wise, John."

Part of teaching discipline to your kids is about learning to trust them—you can't, won't, and shouldn't stand over them with a stick throughout their lives. Your trust in your child will allow her to trust herself.

BEING YOUR CHILD'S ALLY

True discipline always includes love and affection. Your child needs to know that you love him no matter what mistakes he makes or how angry you are at him.

Love is essential for self-respect, and self-respect is key to success. It's your job to help build your children's self-respect by being an ally and standing up for them when they need it. If your kid fears that your love, respect, and acceptance depend upon her actions, she'll become dishonest, she'll hide, and she'll pull away. She needs to know that she can rely on you to be her ally—not to laugh at her, insult her, or love her less—even when she's angry, frightened, or has done something wrong. Be open to your children—the aspects you do like as well as the ones you don't—and they will stay open to you. A kid who is shown respect, who is trusted, and who is led with gentle guidance will grow to be a respectful, trustworthy individual who likes, respects, and believes in herself—and in others.

THE LEAST YOU NEED TO KNOW

◆ Raising a responsible child without being a tyrant means learning effective discipline.

◆ Good discipline is about teaching, not punishment.

◆ Pay attention: Listen, talk, and respond. In other words, be present.

◆ Remember, you have influence, not control.

◆ *No matter* what mistakes he makes, or how angry you are at him, your child needs to know that you love him.

The Reasonable Mom

I know you're not Super Mom—nobody is, so quit trying so hard. Super Mom is a modern mythological figure, a woman with the keys to the Cherokee in one hand, a briefcase and cell phone in the other, a multi-million-dollar report in the briefcase, two charming, well-behaved children, a face that never breaks out or wrinkles, washboard abs, and a halo over a head that never suffers a bad hair day. Look, forget about your neighbor Ms. Jones over there with the perfect house, job, car, clothes, and kids. Even if she wasn't a robotic Stepford Wife (which she is—I peeked through the window one night and watched her husband wind her up with a large key), you would hate her anyhow. Right? Her perfection makes the rest of us mortals look bad. Give it up. Be Reasonable Mom instead.

IT'S A BIRD, IT'S A PLANE, IT'S...

...Reasonable Mom! Who is that masked woman? Well, for one thing, even though she's not perfect, Reasonable Mom tries hard.

She sets reasonable limits, provides reasonable consequences, and she's reasonably consistent about it (yes, even the most reasonable among us makes mistakes!). She tries to model the behavior she'd like to see in her kids. She defines her expectations and disciplinary goals for herself—and her family—at reasonable levels. She knows that change takes time, and she gives herself and her kids a break. She even takes reasonably good care of her own needs. In the rest of this chapter, I'll talk about some of Reasonable Mom's traits—and the reasonable reasons for them.

LIMITS, CONSISTENCY, AND CONSEQUENCES

Most kids do better when there's structure in their lives—when they understand which kinds of behavior are acceptable and which are not, when they know they have boundaries and support they can rely on, and when they know what will happen if they push the boundaries too far. I'm not talking about control, I'm not talking about dominance, I'm talking about limits, consistency, and consequences.

Limits are simply the boundaries of acceptable behavior. Some are set by nature (you can't fly), some are set by the state (you can't drive 100 mph or kill somebody), and some are set by you. It's up to you to define what your family considers acceptable or unacceptable behavior. *Consistency* means applying the same rules for the same results over time, and *consequences* are the good or bad results of a behavior (not to be confused with punishment!).

Introducing…Limits!

Kids need, want, crave limits—so long as they're fair, reasonable, and clearly articulated. For many moms, setting limits—and sticking to them—is the hardest part of parenting. Sometimes it's hard to say no. Hey, no doubt about it, it's hard to deny your child something she really wants. Try to remember (before you give in yet again) that limits will make her feel secure and more confident.

Let's think about it another way. Inside each person, bones supply the support and structure for the body. Without bones, your muscles would have nothing to flex against, and you would dissolve into puddles of floppy flesh—not a very pretty image. Without bones, how would you get anything done? And as the rest of your body grows, so grow your bones.

Outside the body, the limits that you set for your kids provide the same kind of support and structure. Just as the bones grow alongside the muscles, blood, and brain, the limits and boundaries need to expand as your kid grows. They can't stay static.

Much of Reasonable Mom's magic powers come because she knows how to set effective and reasonable limits. I'll talk more—much more—about limits in Chapter 6.

Consistency

Consistency means sameness—it's part of the structure of setting family rules. Consistency is, well, consistent. It's not based on your moods or your whims of the moment. Math works because it's consistent—if 1 + 1 sometimes equaled 2 and sometimes equaled 3, computers wouldn't run, engineers would have nervous break-downs, and all of Western civilization would collapse into a big pile of rubble. (I have days when I think that wouldn't be such a bad thing!) The point is, math is reliable because it's consistent. Discipline also works because it's consistent.

Being consistent often requires a little thinking in advance—"How *do* we want to deal with the issue of _____ ?" If there's a family rule that Marie has to be dressed and breakfasted by 8:30 if she wants to play in her room before school, then no matter how much Marie begs, whines, and pleads that she "just didn't hear the alarm clock," she will have to wait until after school to play with her toys. If Joe knows that if he wants to have friends over, he needs to straighten his room, then either the room is straightened, or Joey plays alone in filth and rubble. Don't set a rule, limit, or consequence *unless* you're going to be consistent in enforcing it.

Being consistent is hard. Kids know instinctually how to manipulate. From the time they're very petite, kids know how to tweak the emotional buttons of adults—it begins as a survival tac-tic, and it's appropriate. Think about it—human babies are weak; they need everything done for them. They have to rely on adult attention to get fed, washed, clothed, and cared for. They know from birth how to get this attention. Fast-forward a few years and picture that cute, dewy-eyed look that Sarah *still* gets as she begs for another cupcake or pleads to be able to attend Rosa's slumber party. (I know a few adults who have fine-tuned this skill—not that I'm about to name any names!)

For some moms, consistency is hard because they were raised by strongly authoritarian parents and want to make up for the sins of the previous generation. Look, all moms want to please. I know you want your kids to love you. You want to be nice; you don't want to come off as an authoritarian. Are you a sucker for a trembling lower lip, big, dewy eyes, and statements such as, "Oh come on, Mom, pleeeease?" Do you ever respond, "Okay, but just this once"? DON'T DO IT!

Kids *need* consistency. I'll go back to my analogy of the body. If you can't rely on your bones being there to support your body when you take a step, after a few uncomfortable splats you're gonna find yourself unwilling to *move*. Your kids are relying on you to be solid in a sometimes fluid world. You're being firm (no, not tough, firm!) for their sake.

It's Also for *Your* Sake!

Being consistent is in your own best interests, as well as your child's.

- ◆ If you set limits or consequences and then give in on them, your kids will learn that you can be pushed into compliance. Then you get whiny Willie.

- ◆ Being consistent is good for your own self-esteem. Nobody wants to be a pushover.

- ◆ It's best to make your rules consistent (and reasonable) for another reason—you! Part of being fair means that you have to follow the family rules, too—that's part of retaining your family's respect.

ALL IN THE FAMILY

Consistency is more than limits and what happens when you exceed them—it's the reliability of a weekly schedule, bedtime being at the same time each night, or the tofu scramble the family eats for breakfast every Saturday before basketball practice. It almost doesn't matter what the routine is—consistency gives everybody something to rely on.

Discipline and consistency go together like donuts and coffee. You'll see your best results when you're consistent with your limits and responses. But consistency is a general parenting technique, not just for matters of misbehavior. If you promise a trip to the local amusement park or chocolate pudding for dessert, then *do it.* Don't promise it unless you're going to deliver. Consistency builds trust.

Consequences

Setting limits on behavior is fine, but what does Reasonable Mom do when those limits are exceeded? (Warning: Your child is approaching the speed of light!) Reasonable Mom relies on reasonable consequences to misbehavior.

Let's get one thing straight: Consequences are no way, no how the same as punishment. Consequences are more like gravity—if you drop a pizza, it falls. You've gotta get it in the kid's head that if she does this, that happens. "If I do my homework, I get a good grade. If I don't do my homework, I'm gonna get a bad grade. Ooh, cool." Consequences can be "natural" (if you never feed the parakeet, it will die) or "logical" (if you punch people, they're going to be unhappy with you), pleasant or unpleasant. They're simply the outcome of an event or a course of events.

Like gravity, Reasonable Mom's consequences are applied consistently. I'll talk about finding appropriate consequences to misbehavior in Chapter 7.

> **WISE WORDS**
>
> *Limits* are behavior boundaries. *Consistency* means same-ness—the same rules and results over time. *Consequences* are what happens as a result of a behavior—good or bad.

"DON'T %&*$% CURSE AT *ME*, YOUNG LADY!"

Monkey see, monkey do, and that goes for children, too. If you want your child to act in certain ways, the best disciplinary method is modeling the correct behavior. Words, if they aren't followed up by actions, have no teeth.

If Mom Lisa, who despises mornings, slams her bedroom door and growls like a grumpy bear as she enters the kitchen for break-fast, how can she expect her kids to walk as though on air, close doors gently, and greet the world with a smile on their shiny faces? Lisa has a double standard. As much as she growls, "Do as I say, not as I do," it's just not gonna wash with her kids.

Negative Modeling

When you start defining family limits, one of the things to keep in mind is you. If you limit your 13-year-old to 10-minute showers in the morning, you'd better not practice your own A.M. bathroom arias for an hour each day. Say you forbid your kid to curse but your language makes a grizzled old sailor sound innocent. What's going to happen when your kid gets out on the playground? (You #*$&#$ guessed it!)

If rules are made to be kept for the kids and broken by you, you're giving some pretty iffy messages: I'm in power, you're not. I'm an adult so I matter, you're a kid so you don't. When you grow up you can break all the rules and it doesn't matter.

Some rules, obviously, are only for the kids, just like some (such as no butter on that second roll) are only for you. *Of course* you don't have to do your homework between 7 and 8 every night.

MOM KNOWS BEST

Does the occasional *!&*& slip out in your family? One mom told her kids, "Those are family words. We don't use them around other people. They're angry words, and if we use them around other people, we will bring trouble on ourselves."

Positive Modeling

It's more than what you don't do, it's what you do and who you are. You set your standards by example. If you're struggling with a certain behavior, let your kid see that, too. It will help her see that though you're not perfect, you're constantly striving to improve.

Modeling Communication Skills

Part of modeling behavior is modeling appropriate and effective ways of communicating. A family who communicates well has fewer problems than a family who doesn't. Sometimes it's hard, but don't stress: Chapter 5 is all about communication strategies and skills for talking with and listening to your kids.

THE GENTLE APPROACH TO DISCIPLINE

Most disciplinary situations can, and should be, handled by gentle techniques. I'll be talking more about positive discipline in Chapter 4, but as you begin the process of transforming yourself from Wicked Witch of the West to Reasonable Mom, here are a few things to keep in mind to prevent—and fix—disciplinary problems:

◆ Encourage.

◆ Use humor.

◆ Be considerate.

◆ Show affection.

◆ Put in the time and energy.

◆ Be patient.

◆ Be fair.

◆ Don't sweat the small stuff.

◆ Calm mom, happy child.

"Go Girl!"—Encourage

Children thrive on encouragement. Encouragement should be specific, deliberate, and frequent. Take time to notice—every day—the things your child is doing right. Take time to point out things you're particularly proud of. ("Susan, I noticed the way you helped Mrs. Robins by reaching for the can of corned beef hash at the store today—you saw she was having trouble and just stepped in without being asked.")

Use encouragement when you see improvement in a situation. ("I see you're working hard on your throwing. I know you're going to be able to get a place on the team this year.") Later in the book, I'll talk more about encouragement and how you can use it.

WISE WORDS

Encouragement is a form of positive reinforcement that focuses on a child's efforts—rather than results—and helps a child become self-motivated: "You can do it," "You seem to like that," "You really worked hard on that," "What do you think of what you did?"

Use Humor

Mom's Motto #167: It's better to laugh than scream. Being firm with limits and consequences does not mean wandering through the house with a mean and horrid look. If you've got a choice, it's better to see the humor in a situation. Tension is often defused by laughter. Laughing doesn't mean you don't take something seriously. Humor is a great way to keep a sense of perspective about things (look, you may not like them, but food fights are not a capital crime).

MOM ALWAYS SAID

Sarcasm is *not* an effective or kind use of humor. Sarcasm bites, cuts, and stings. Keep your humor gentle, Mom. Laugh with your child, not at her.

Be Considerate

This is a modeling issue, as well as one of general respect. It's simple, really: Be who you want your kids to emulate.

Show Affection

Hug, hug, hug. Yes, even those gawky adolescents who are beginning to tower over you and might half-heartedly push you away with a "Gross, Mom." It's their job to act cool, it's yours to love them to bits. It's the warm glow they'll remember and count on when the world seems cold and sharp. Gentle guidance delivered with a hug and a smooch will be accepted far better than guidance delivered in a cold, uncaring manner.

Put in the Time and Energy

Finding time to just hang with your kids can be a real challenge—and rather guilt-provoking given everybody's busy schedules these days. Part of it is prioritizing—spend an hour with Jerry, helping with his homework, working on an art project, or playing a board game, instead of an hour watching Jerry Seinfeld. When you're in touch with your kid, you'll be more able to see problems coming and halt them in their tracks before they darken your door.

Be Patient

Give change a chance. Rome wasn't built in a day, and you're not going to turn into Reasonable Mom overnight. (Stepping into a phone booth and whipping off your clothes probably won't work either.) It takes time to learn new patterns.

It will also take time for your kid to change habits. Part of becoming Reasonable Mom is being reasonable—allowing a reasonable amount of time for change to occur, and having a reasonable response when it doesn't happen immediately, or without resistance. Here's the bad news (thought I'd wait till now to spring it on you!): Taking a positive approach to discipline can be slow going. There are no quick fixes. Here's the good news: This stuff works and works and works forever. By using encouragement, setting limits, and providing reasonable consequences, you're helping your child develop self-control *and* self-respect.

Don't give up on your child—or on yourself. Sometimes behavior takes months or years to change. That doesn't mean you're failing, or that it isn't worth trying to change. Stay the course, ma'am! Transmit hope!

Be Fair

"But Mom, that's not fair!" How many times have you heard that one? Kids are deeply aware of injustices. Reasonable Mom does her best to be fair and just (they're not always the same thing, as you know full well if you have more than one child). She probably succeeds most of the time, but sometimes she may not communicate fairness clearly. Jonah doesn't understand why he must come right home from school. He's chronically late because he's mad—he thinks you don't trust him. You do trust him, you're just worried about an increase in violence in your neighborhood. Oops! Time for a talk. And a listen.

MOM ALWAYS SAID

Are you being reasonable? Watch your kid! If your kid is acting angry and rebellious about a limit you've set, maybe the limit is too stringent, or maybe your reasons for it are unclear.

Don't Sweat the Small Stuff

You're not going to win every battle; you don't even need to fight them all! Actually, a discipline situation isn't really a battle at all. In a battle, one person wins, another loses. This isn't your goal. When you teach discipline, you're trying to strengthen your child and help form her character—not prove that you're stronger.

This means choosing your situations—and sometimes choosing *not* to mention it when the kid is breaking "the rules." Don't sweat the small stuff—save it for when it *really* matters.

When you relax a bit with the discipline thing and are willing to let small stuff slide, you free yourself to be able to *enjoy* your child again and have some fun! Fun is good! Think about what you were doing the last time your kid turned to you and said, "Mom, this is *fun!*" Then, do it again!

Calm Mom, Happy Child

A big part of becoming Reasonable Mom is taking care of yourself. Yes, you there with the high stress level! Does this ever happen to you? You're driving down the freeway in a rush to pick up Sally at basketball practice and get her to the orthodontist on time and you think, "I need some more serenity in my life." So, you turn on the classical music station. Now you're driving madly, avoiding the slow idiot in the right lane, avoiding an accident in the left, one eye on the road, one eye on the gas tank indicator, one eye on the clock on the dashboard, but you're calm. The classical music is lovely. Suddenly you realize, "Oh no! Now I'm multi-tasking my serenity!"

When the world feels overwhelming, when you feel like you're spending your life just trying to get everything done and the bills paid, too, you're gonna have a hard time being Reasonable Mom. Instead, you're probably going to be cranky. Any little thing will get that temper flaring—and you might take it out on the kid. I'll remind you, Mom, this is probably not conducive to effective discipline. Here are some suggestions for self-nurturing:

◆ *Make yourself a success list.* Next time you're at the store, pick up one of those eeny tiny notebooks—usually 59¢ or less (you can afford it)—and, before you drop into bed exhausted, write down three things that you did well each and every day.

Large or small, acknowledging your own successes will make you feel better about your own life. One day your list might read: (1) closed million-dollar real estate deal, (2) washed cat without getting major lacerations, and (3) bought Laura a jacket that she *liked*. Another day your list might read: (1) got up on time, (2) didn't eat candy bar when offered, and (3) flossed.

MOM KNOWS BEST

The task is not to multi-task your serenity, but to serenitize your multi-tasking. Breathe and relax. Are you up for the challenge?

♦ *Set small goals every day.* Take 30 seconds before you fling your-self out of bed in the morning to set a couple of tiny goals—things you *know* you can achieve. (I *will* call for Tony's check-up. I *will* water the orchid in the bathroom.)

♦ *Reduce your stress, anxiety, guilt, and fear.* "Yeah right, Mom." No, I mean it, and do it the *physical* way. A bath, a walk, a mas-sage, a dance class, a trip to the gym, good sex, a foot soak, a slowly savored glass of cool water on a hot day. Even if you have *no* time for yourself, you can still take 10 long, deep breaths. In through the nose, out through the mouth, in through the nose, out through the mouth. Try to relax those shoulders. Not to get too cosmic about it, but you *are* (at least in part) your body, and when your body is happy, so are you.

♦ *Celebrate yourself.* Don't denigrate your victories—no matter how small. Some moms do affirmations (I'm a wonderful per-son!), and some just try to enjoy a little of who they are, every day.

YOU ARE THE MOM

You are the Big Mamoo, the sturdy support, the tall wall of mother. Every kid—everybody—needs a caretaker who will provide encouragement, guidance, limits, and unconditional love. In Barbara Kingsolver's novel, *The Bean Trees*, Taylor, the narrator, says that her mother always expected the best from her, and that no matter what Taylor did, her mother acted, "...like it was the moon I had just hung up in the sky and plugged in all the stars. Like I was that good." As far as I'm concerned, all moms should strive to be that kind of mother to their children.

Kids Are Good Company

Discipline doesn't work if you're removed, cool, and dictating from on high. Work to develop a companionship with your kids. Find things you like to do together (check out the special time section in Chapter 4), go on steady dates, and take spur of the moment shopping trips. Tell them about your lousy day and ask for their input. If you take the time to develop a companionship and if you and your kid are comfortable talking with each other, you'll have a foundation of trust to carry you through the rocky rebellious years looming ahead. ("Look out! It's a giant hormone! DUCK!!!!!")

She's Not Your Confidante

"She's my best friend." Melissa says that about her 10-year-old daughter, Samantha. "She's so much fun to play with, and be with, and we talk to each other about everything." Sounds great. Just what I was talking about. Or is it? If you talk to Samantha, you'll hear a slightly different story: "Yeah, my mom relies on me a lot. She's going through kind of a hard time right now...."

The look on Samantha's face says it all—it's the look of a child trying to be a grown-up, carrying the weight of all her mother's problems. She feels a responsibility—and it's more responsibility than she should need to carry. She's your kid and your companion, but not your confidante. When things are tough, you've got to be the adult—it's not about pretending to be somebody you're not or putting on a happy face when you feel sad. You can, and should, be real and human, but get your therapy elsewhere.

MOM KNOWS BEST

Want to be respected? Here are three phrases to *purge* from your vocabulary: "Do as I say, not as I do," "Because I say so, that's why," and "Shut up."

TRUST YOUR CHILD

Discipline is, ultimately, self-discipline, and you're gonna have to let your kid go and just trust that what you've taught has been implanted deep in that small body. Like it or not, you're not always there and you're not always going to be. Trust internalizes the discipline. Take a leap of faith—the more you show your trust, the more your child will strive to meet it. Kids, like moms, strive to be reasonable, too.

THE LEAST YOU NEED TO KNOW

- ◆ Nobody is perfect. Strive to be reasonable instead.
- ◆ Limits, consistency, and consequences are essential for effective discipline.
- ◆ What you do and say matters—model the behavior you would like to see in your child.
- ◆ A gentle, positive approach to discipline is more effective than a harsh, negative approach.
- ◆ *You* are the authority figure.
- ◆ If you trust your child, she will learn to trust herself.

The Reasonable Child

"WELL, HOW ABOUT A VERY SMALL ELEPHANT?"

In the last chapter, you learned to take perfection, dump it in the garbage, take the garbage to the dump, and reset your goals to reasonable. Just as you don't expect yourself to be perfect, you shouldn't expect your kids to be perfect, either. Sometimes it's hard to know what levels of expectation you *should* expect. This chapter focuses on that lovely little beast, the Reasonable Child.

Here's my warning to you: This chapter is filled with generalizations. Hey, kids are individuals, and since I don't know *your* kid, I'm going to *have* to generalize. All throughout this book I'm going to talk about things that may not ever apply to your kid and things that applied to your kid last year. But though I may not know your child, you do. You'll know it when I hit the nail on the head. ("Owwwwwww!!!")

WHO IS THIS REASONABLE CHILD?

The Reasonable Child is not perfect. The Reasonable Child is child-ish, and I don't mean that in a bad way. He's a kid, you know! He tests limits, gets wild, rebels, and then surprises you with acts of kindness, affection, and sudden sweetness.

What Does He Want, Anyway?

The Reasonable Child wants what all people want—to feel loved, needed, and encouraged to be himself, with his individual person-ality quirks and temperament. When you love him for who he is, he'll feel self-confident enough to grow, stretch, and challenge the world! I can't stress the importance of love, encouragement, and approval enough. A child who believes his parents are disappoint-ed in him will lose confidence, and his development may slow.

ALL IN THE FAMILY

These middle years of childhood between young child and full-fledged adolescent are often considered the "easy" years. Some parents are lulled into inaction during this period, unaware that their kids still need direction, lim-its, and attention—the discipline that will help build their confi-dence so they'll make it through their teen years intact.

ASSESSING "REASONABLE" BEHAVIOR

Here's a question from the old mail bag: "Hey Mom, how do I know if a certain behavior is normal or abnormal, if it is, in fact, 'reason-able' behavior?"

Okay, this is a hard one. There's no easy answer. You'll have to look at the child's age, development, and temperament.

Ages and Stages

Remember way back when your baby was just born? Maybe you had a friend whose infant was a couple months older than yours.

How different in age your babies seemed. With a baby, you always know pretty much what's going to come next. There are behavior and growth charts up the wazoo. You can anticipate almost to the month when Junior will start to babble or learn to eat with a spoon.

Older kids are different. The next time you visit your child's school, check out the amazing diversity of kids in the sixth grade. Even among kids the same age you'll find a range of emotional, social, intellectual, and physical development. Small, skinny kids sit next to hulking dudes who have reached their full height. Math geniuses are next to kids who are still mastering long division.

Another thing to keep in mind is that development—and maturity—might be uneven for different qualities. The littlest kid might be the most emotionally and intellectually mature kid in the school. The hulkster might still be snuggling his blankey each night.

Focus on your child's positive personality traits. When you need to talk about negative behaviors (and you may need to less often than you think), stay specific. Positive or negative, what you say has a strange way of being self-reinforcing. Focusing on the positive helps put negative traits in perspective and helps you enjoy your kid more. You'll be surprised how much better she'll respond.

Don't "type" your child. While his current personality and temperamental traits might be permanent, they may also be temporary—a "phase." How your child is developing can affect his behavior, and vice versa, and your own parenting style and the overall environment can affect his behavior and development, too.

Given these disclaimers, I find it reassuring to look at the age "profiles" I've compiled below from the work of child development experts (see the reading list in the back of this book). Keep in mind that these profiles aren't exact—your child might "blend" into the year ahead and the year behind at the same time. But sometimes, when your child is a total beast, it helps to be able to take a step back and say, "Ah well, at least it's age appropriate."

A Few Gross Generalizations

The Eight-Year-Old

The eight-year-old is stretching out into the world. This is the year when the child loses her primary dependence on you, her parent, and begins to develop a more realistic view of you (warts, wrinkles, pimples, and all!). Some eight-year-olds may still be afraid of the dark. Boys and girls still share interests, but they're becoming more aware of gender differences. Both boys and girls may suddenly begin to ask detailed questions about birth, marriage, and sex, but in a factual, investigative manner. In general, eight is a good year. The eight-year-old is self-confident, considerate, and cooperative. For the eight-year-old, rules are very important—she relies on them and might flip out if you fold, spindle, or mutilate them. "That's not fair!" is her battle cry. Woe to the hypocritical parent! You're gonna get it!

The Nine-Year-Old

The nine-year-old shows even more self-confidence and independence. Hanging out with the nine-year-old is fun! He's a pleasant companion. He's very cool. He's also deeply involved with his friends; sometimes he seems not to need you at all. He may complain that you "treat him like a child" (and it will do you little good to remind him that he is). There's lots of illness and aches and pains in the "typical" nine-year-old's life. The nine-year-old has a new awareness of the reproductive aspects of sex. That often means lots of snickering and dirty jokes.

The 10-Year-Old

Ten has long been known as the "climax" of childhood. The typical 10-year-old loves herself and her family. She's cooperative. This is, however, the last age for sometime when she will fully enjoy going on a family outing. She still needs a lot of supervision and direction. She loves messes, has to be coerced to bathe, and hates to make her bed. At 10, a child begins to "take stock" of her faults and assets. She constantly joins clubs and "loves" organized activities. Girls tend to like smaller peer groups. Excluding other girls is a common occurrence. Ten-year-old boys tend to get along better with each other than do 10-year-old girls. The 10-year-old has a strict moral code with a strong sense of justice, but she's more concerned about what's wrong than what's right, and she still relies on her parents to double-check her perceptions.

The 11-Year-Old and the 12-Year-Old

Wow! It's a preadolescent! "Look at her wrong—or sometimes just look at her—and she runs down the hall to her room and flings herself on the bed, sobbing," says one mom. These are the "transition" years between childhood and adolescence, filled with stress and anticipation. Some kids are deeply aware—and have great trepidation—about leaving childhood behind. One girl dreamed of visiting a park where she used to play. She was aware that she couldn't go on the merry-go-round—it was off-limits. She woke with deep sense of loss.

The 11- or 12-year-old is very often awful to be around. He's defiant, grumpy, and moody. There is a resurgence of "bathroom humor" in boys, which has to do with anxious feelings around newly felt sexual feelings. Schoolwork is not as gratifying for boys as it was for them when they were eight or nine or ten. (Girls are often better students than boys at this age.) The 11- or 12-year-old may actively refuse to do chores, and he'll yell at his parents and siblings at the drop of a hat. He's emotionally spontaneous and completely unaware of the havoc he's causing. Despite all this, family life is still very important to him. Girls especially form intense—and sometimes brutal—relationships with each other at this age. All is not lost; things will get better.

The 13-Year-Old

The 13-year-old is introspective and temperamental. He's sensitive, he's private, he's protecting his new personality like a flower. Thirteen is known as "the tear year." Thirteen is sad. Thirteen is touchy. Thirteen has "crushes" on teachers, older neighbors, and cute movie stars. The 13-year-old spends a lot of time in his room.

The 14-Year-Old

The 14-year-old is pretty cool and contented. She's regained some of her equilibrium and can be quite pleasant to be around, unless you're one of her parents. In which case, "Suffer!" You've seen that disgusted look and heard the 14-year-old's constant mantra, "Moom!!!!" You can't do a thing right. Give it up and wait. Here's the good news: At 15 they start becoming human again.

NO TWO ALIKE (ADJUST ACCORDINGLY)

When you're trying to figure out whether certain behaviors are reasonable and what kind of expectations you should set, take your kid, the one standing right there in front of you, into consideration. Every child is born with her own temperament—witness the story of two siblings I know, Laid-Back Larry and High-Powered Harry. Same parents, same family, same influences. Yet from the time they were born, they approached the world in entirely different ways. The key difference? Temperament.

The Nine Characteristics of Temperament

All of us are born with tendencies to act and react to incidents and people in specific ways. These tendencies—and they are only that, tendencies—are called *temperament*. Here are the nine temperamental markers to help you figure out what's going on with your child:

◆ *Energy level.* Is the child's energy level high or low? Is he constantly on the go, or does he sit quietly?

◆ *Regularity.* Is the child regular or irregular in her sleep patterns, eating, and other bodily functions?

◆ *First reaction.* When the child is presented with a new situation, does he jump right in, or does he hold back a while before participating?

◆ *Adaptability.* Does the child adapt quickly to change, or does she get upset by surprises? How flexible is she?

◆ *Intensity.* How strong are the child's emotional reactions? Is he "hot" or "cool"?

◆ *Mood.* Is the child basically happy and content, or is she generally "down" or cranky?

◆ *Persistence.* Does the person have an easy or difficult time switching activities? Does he "beat a dead horse"?

◆ *Perceptiveness.* How aware is the child of her environment—the colors, noises, people, and objects around her?

◆ *Sensitivity.* How sensitive—on a physical level—is the child? Is he highly aware of noises, scratchy clothing, smells, tastes, or temperature?

WISE WORDS

Temperament refers to the way a person approaches the world. It includes things such as energy level, regularity, first reaction, adaptability, intensity, mood, persistence, perceptiveness, and sensitivity.

Some kids are naturally more "easy"—calm and positive—and some are more "difficult"—fussy as babies, prone to tantrums, high-energy, moody. Some are "slow to warm up"—shy, reluctant to face new situations. None of these inborn temperaments or personality traits are bad, they're just a piece of who your kid is. Every person—yes, you, too, Mom—has a variety of traits that can be labeled "easy" or "difficult." Try to think of your child's temperament in objective terms. When you do that, you can separate a bit from your emotional reactions.

Problem or Temperament?

When you're assessing your child for "reasonable" behavior, take temperament into consideration and adjust your expectations to meet his capabilities. If you're having constant battles with Pierre to get him to be more polite and quit mumbling, stop and reassess. Is shyness part of his nature? Is he really being rude, or is he just uncomfortable? How can you help him feel less anxious?

If Latifa is having trouble finishing her homework before dinner, perhaps she's *not* lazy. Maybe she's a thoughtful, persistent, thorough child who must stick to a task and think through concepts before writing about them. She might need more time to do her work or need help learning how to prioritize.

It's Not Fixed in Stone

Your child was born with certain temperamental tendencies, but she's not fixed for life. You can work to change things—channel her high energy into enthusiasm or foster his sensitivity into empathy and creative work.

When Temperaments Clash

If you have a child whose temperament is very different from yours, take solace. Nothing is wrong with your child. You're not inadequate as a parent. You simply are very different people in some ways, and there are lots of ways of being in this world. When you realize that your kid's behavior is—at least in part—a function of her temperament, you'll become more patient. Work with her to increase her range of capabilities, but don't force her to try to be like you. Hey, who said you were perfect, anyway?

LETTING KIDS BE KIDS

The Reasonable Child is unreasonable a lot of the time. The path to learning never runs smooth. Kids make mistakes, and they try and fail, they exasperate with their exuberance, and they bore you with bad jokes. Allow it. Allow for dissent, criticism, and rebellion. Any child with a questioning spirit, a zest for life, and a strong sense of self is going to look for your panic buttons, and then push them. But it's that same spirit, zest, and sense of self that will carry him strongly through life.

You Set 'Em, They Test 'Em

Testing, stretching, pushing, growing, and learning—these are part of your kid's job description. The hardest part—for moms—is that a lot of this testing and pushing happens against you. This is the dynamic you're setting up: You set the rules, they test 'em. It's a natural—and necessary—part of establishing individuality and independence.

Being "bad" sometimes is not only normal, it's healthy. The child is testing your boundaries and his own self-control. Tests are important—if you were a contractor and you hired some workers to build some walls, you'd test the building materials and you'd test the "weight loads" to see how much stress they could take. Kids need to test the structure to see if it can be relied on.

Your job description includes: breathing deeply, keeping cool, and keeping your sense of humor. When your otherwise Reasonable Child is being unreasonable, remember that he's not a *bad* kid. Separate the behavior from the personality—he's a good kid misbehaving.

Walk a Mile in Her Shoes

Step into Alice's shoes—remember your own childhood? What did you like to do as a child? What did you hate? Once you banish the "shoulds" from your thoughts ("My child is eight, she should be putting away her toys") and replace them with some memories of your own childhood, you'll be better able to deal with Alice's dragging feet as she refuses to clean up her room.

Look at Effort, Not Result

Eleven-year-old Selina struggled with her chores of washing the dinner dishes once a week and making her own bed. She hated them, she procrastinated, and the struggle leaked over the whole family. Her parents, Anna and Lee, were tired of nagging, and Selina was frustrated and upset. After a lot of talking, Selina agreed to try again. When Anna checked Selina's room she found that Selina had, indeed, made her bed—if you could call it that. The spread was pulled up over a big lump of blankets. Arghhh! That kid! Yet, considering Selina's struggles, her effort was great progress. She'd made a reasonable stab at it, and a reasonable stab at it counts. For Selina's parents to criticize the quality of her work would be counterproductive. Selina has years to learn how to refine her skills.

Great! Now Chill Out

When you start thinking about a concept like discipline, it's human nature to start seeing it, or the need for it, everywhere. It's like when you buy a car. Until you get a silver hatchback, you have no idea how many of them are on the road. Suddenly, there are hatchbacks everywhere—on the freeway, cutting you off at the red light, near the dry cleaners.... So it is with discipline. Once you start thinking about it, you'll start seeing behavior problems, like silver hatchbacks, everywhere. Chill, Mom. Life is not all discipline. You're probably just sensitized. Don't become the Discipline Queen, picking on every little breach of the rules. Let the kids be free!

LETTING GO

Hey, you're not really in charge here. Or if you are, it's not for long. Parental control is fleeting—if it ever really occurs at all. Parental control is just a momentary step on a child's path to self-control.

If you've ever been around ducks, you know mama duck takes her job of raising her babies seriously. When it's time for them to learn to swim, she's out in front, showing them how it's done. But once those ducklings get in the water, they're on their own. Being human (when last I checked), you don't, of course, throw your young into the big pond with quite the same aplomb. You're there for them. But there comes a time when it's time to find out whether the self-control and discipline has sunk in. Gotta let go. You won't know if it's working until you let the little duck swim.

Let Her Try New Things

You can help your Reasonable Child build self-control and "internalize" the discipline she's learning by giving her more responsibility and allowing her to try new things. Many boundaries set by parents are meant to expand as the child grows—perhaps more allowance, slumber parties, going to the movies alone with friends. The looser the reins, the tighter the surveillance—watch closely, and keep checking in with her to assess how things are going. She's learning responsibility and safety but still needs limits and rules. You're walking a fine line here. Here's the rule: When it comes to safety or values (as your family defines them), *keep those limits firm and explicit!*

Give Them a Chance

Kids ask for more responsibility in a variety of ways, not all of them clear, clean, and openly communicative. Sometimes they ask for it in reverse. Andrew left the refrigerator door open day and night—and "day and night" was how often he was coming into the kitchen, staring into a refrigerator brimming with bounty, and yelling, "Mom! There's nothing to eat!" Andrew—without knowing it—was asking for more responsibility.

Andrew's mom put him in charge of making a shopping list of food and snacks he liked. She provided some guidelines (three items of "healthy" food for each "junk" item) and some limits. (If he orders it, he eats it. If he doesn't make the list, the food doesn't get bought.) She specifically refrained from commenting on his sometimes odd choices (cans of pickled water chestnuts, butterscotch ice cream topping—but no ice cream). Andrew responded well to the increased responsibility. He took the job *very* seriously and began experimenting with cooking interesting, gourmet food for the whole family.

In contrast, here's a story about an approach that didn't work. Melinda, the baby-sitter, told nine-year-old twins Cindy and Mindy that they needed to learn how to resist temptation. She placed a plate of fresh chocolate chip cookies in front of them and said they weren't allowed to eat any. Then she left them alone in the room for half an hour. Melinda was trying to test self-control before she'd taught it. Instead, the kids learned they were weak and that self-control is misery.

MOM KNOW BEST

Mom's Motto #99: Responsibility breeds responsibility. If you want your child to take charge of something, delegate the responsibility to her. Then back off, baby. Let *her* do it.

YOUR CHILD'S EXPECTATIONS

The Reasonable Child will set reasonable expectations for himself— if you help him! As the school-age child grows, he begins to gain some objectivity about himself and about life. You can help him define who he wants to be and how he wants to behave. Keep in mind that your expectations will affect your child's expectations— low or high.

The Perfectionist Child

Some kids tend toward perfectionism. Perfectionism can be very painful for a child. Your child might need your help to realize that, sometimes, "perfect is the enemy of good." Here are clues to identify the Perfectionist Child:

- She gets easily frustrated or quickly gives up on tasks, saying, "I can't do it."

- She's a chronic procrastinator. Many perfectionists are afraid to start a project because they're afraid it won't turn out perfect.

- She has trouble completing tasks. The perfectionist imagines the "fantasy" finished product will be perfect. By keeping it incomplete, she can live with the fantasy, not with the inevitably flawed reality.

Here are some tips to help your child get over the need to be perfect:

- Assess your own expectations—for your child and for yourself. What standards are you setting? Are they realistic? What are you modeling? If you cut your kid some slack but are always on your own case, your child will pick up on that. Try and be easier on yourself.

- Help your child prioritize. If Sally is worried that every homework assignment must be completely perfect, she'll have a hard time getting *any* of it done. Sit with her, make a list of tasks, and talk about which ones are most important.

- Show your own imperfections and help your child see that *nobody* is perfect all the time. Use examples of mistakes you've made and times you've failed, flailed, bombed out, and bit the big one. You're still surviving and thriving today, right?

The Child Who's Not Self-Motivated

"He has no ambition, no goals; he doesn't think he can *do* anything!" The first two parts of this parent's complaint don't, in themselves, present a concern. A lot of kids lack "ambition" and "goals" because they're deeply involved in being children and unworried about the future. That's healthy; a kid like this could just be easygoing and emotionally secure. There's lots of time. All too soon, he'll be plunged deeply into the dog-eat-dog quality of this society.

The last part of this parent's complaint, "...he doesn't think he can *do* anything!" is the kicker. A kid who doesn't feel successful will often stop trying, and he'll give in to despair or depression. Check out your kid. Are his lack of goals and ambition coming from an easy nature or from a lack of self-confidence? What can you do to help your child feel more successful in this world?

Here's an idea: Provide opportunities to stretch and try things. Sports teams, dance classes, science club, band, circus training, 4-H programs, drama—these kinds of activities can help a child gain a sense of her own abilities and accomplishments. It's an investment. If your kid feels good about one ability—no matter what it is— she'll do better in *all* areas of her life.

MOM KNOWS BEST

Mom says, "Success spreads." If your child is having fun and developing skills in drama or sports, his self-image will benefit and you'll notice the difference.

What the Reasonable Child Expects

The Reasonable Child expects you to love her, enjoy her, and appreciate her for who she is. The Reasonable Child wants you to show your pride (even when she's squirming and saying, "Moom!"). The Reasonable Child is reasonably sure that you're on her side; that if she comes to you in big trouble, you'll calmly help her find her way out of trouble; that you'll be fair, though not too lenient; and that you'll give her the support and boundaries she needs.

THE SELF-RESPECTING CHILD

The relationship between the love of parents and self-respect is widely recognized. I'm assuming all parents love their children (those who don't won't be reading this book). The most important factor is how you show your love. Yes, I'm talking about unconditional love. Unconditional love promotes self-acceptance and self-confidence. The child who knows she's loved, who is encouraged, who is praised for what she does well, and who has experiences of mastery and success will grow to respect and cherish herself and be able to make positive choices in her life.

Security Against Future Harm

All this discipline and attention is aimed at raising a clear-thinking child. You can't protect a child from the dangers of the world—dangers are all around us. Unless you're the president or a celebrity with major security issues, you can't—and shouldn't—provide a set of bodyguards to protect your child all through life. Besides, even Uzi-bearing bodyguards can't provide security against cracked confidence, a broken heart, depression, or poor lifestyle choices. A child's protection will ultimately come from within. All you can do is teach him that he can make choices and show him how to develop the tools to do it. That's his armor, Mom. Invisible, but strong.

THE LEAST YOU NEED TO KNOW

- ◆ Kids are never going to be perfect. Adjust your expectations to "reasonable."

- ◆ You can assess if your child is being "reasonable" by looking at her age, development, and temperament.

- ◆ Unconditional love helps raise a child who is self-confident, compassionate, and respectful.

Positive Discipline

Okay, Reasonable Mom and Reasonable Child, how about this discipline thing? Back in Chapter 1, I defined discipline as "...the process of instilling values in your child through example, encouragement, and gentle guidance." Cool. But how do you instill those values?

WHAT IS POSITIVE DISCIPLINE?

"Bring Jesse down to the Valu-Tune shop today, will you, Maude? He's due for a morality tune-up. Could you also have them check his manners quotient? I think it may be running a little low."

Alas and alack, kids aren't like cars. You can't pour in self-control from a can. Most kids are missing a little hatch in the back of the head that can be opened to insert a values chip.

My approach—and the approach of many experts in the field of child development—is to use positive discipline as part of daily life.

Positive discipline concentrates on preventing problems. Positive discipline is *not* a whack on the butt and "Get to your room young man!" It's also *not* the "too-groovy-for-words" approach of ignoring misbehavior, smiling benignly, and banning the word "No!"

Instead, it teaches kids how to make their own choices and to understand the consequences of their choices. When necessary, it provides related, respectful, and reasonable responses to misbehavior. If you teach positive discipline to your children, you should never have to resort to punishment.

WISE WORDS

Positive discipline is an approach to discipline that incorporates encouragement, praise, trust, and respect for children through firm, wise limits.

Here are some of the tenets and traits of positive discipline as I use it.

Teaching Your Values

Magnets are cool. Take two plain magnets (no, not ones that are already decorating your refrigerator that have stuff pasted on one side). Put one in each hand and bring your hands slowly together. As the magnets approach each other, you'll either suddenly feel a little pull as they attract each other or a little push as they repel each other.

Kids are like magnets. Depending upon which way they're polarized, positive or negative, they'll either attract or repel the values they're exposed to. That's why I go for the positive approach to discipline.

If you stay positive in your general approach to your kids, most of your value-instilling work will be done automatically. Now *that's* cool. (If you're too negative all the time, your kid, like the magnet, will be repelled.)

Fostering Mutual Respect

Positive discipline teaches respect by honoring the child with the same. Some people call it karma, some call it the Golden Rule ("do unto others"), some listen to Mom. We all have the same message on this one—you get as good as you give. You want some respect? Show some respect. Yeah, your kid is smaller than you and not as hairy. He's still an individual human being, deserving of the same level of honor and respect you are. And since kids learn by imitation, just demonstrating respectful behavior will take you a long way.

Here are some ways to show your child respect:

◆ Respect her body and personal space.

◆ Respect her temperament.

◆ Respect her privacy.

◆ Respect her opinions.

Respecting your kids doesn't mean agreeing with everything they say, do, or believe. Nor does it mean letting them run wild in the mistaken belief that they always know what's right for them. Respect just acknowledges that a child's feelings and beliefs are valid. Respect uses that acknowledgment as a starting place, and then moves forward from there.

Positive Reinforcement

Look, all people, especially children, want to please. The desire for approval is universal. In our society, most of us focus on our kid's negative behavior. You expect your kids to behave. When they don't, you get mad at them. But what happens when you notice and comment on the "good" behavior, too? When a kid feels noticed and validated, the "good" behavior is likely to increase and the "bad" behavior will decrease.

Positive discipline uses positive reinforcement—encouragement, rewards, descriptive praise—as an impetus for preventing and changing misbehavior and maintaining and increasing good behavior. In Chapter 6, I'll talk about specific "reinforcers" you can use. Don't stress out—positive reinforcement isn't the only trick

Mom's got in her bag. It does happen to be a *great*—and common—trick. What do you think grades in school are about? Jennifer does well and is reinforced with an A, and Mom gets a bumper sticker with "My Child is on the Honor Role at Central Elementary" to decorate the back of the minivan. (Think about it, you respond to positive reinforcement, too! How about that year-end bonus at work?)

MOM ALWAYS SAID

If you use praise as a positive reinforcement, make sure it's descriptive. Instead of saying, "What a smart girl I have," say, "I see you did an excellent job on your math test." General praise only tells the child that she needs to please you.

Using Choices

Back when the kids were mere toddlers, you may remember providing choices such as, "Which kind of juice do you want, apple or cranberry?" Providing choices to older kids is a little more complex, but often as effective. ("John, you can choose to go to the family party with us, or you can stay home and clean your room.") Life is a series of choices. Helping your kids learn the skills to make appropriate, positive choices in their lives is part of parenting well. In Chapter 6, I'll talk explicitly about using choices to prevent problems and teach your children internal discipline.

TAKE SOME TIME TOGETHER

"Ack! Late, late, late! No time for chatting, no time for fun. Gotta run, hurry up, no time for a chat." Does this sound familiar? Does this sound like you? Are you dozing through too many meetings, drinking too much coffee, and spending way too much time bopping down the highway with the kids, the neighbor kids, and the barking dog in the back? When was the last time you just chilled with the kids? Hey pal, it's hard to compete with the TV, CD player, and ringing telephone—they're just too noisy! Part of positive discipline comes from making time for it to happen. Mom says it's time for ("Drum roll, Charley!") family time, family meetings, and special time!

Family time, family meetings, and special time are problem-prevention as well as problem-solving activities. If you want to get fancy about it, you can call these your "communication forums." They are important, and not just when Chrissie is crying or Joshua is a jerk.

Family time and family meetings are group activities. It doesn't matter if your family numbers 2 or 20, you're all included, you're all invited, and nobody is excused for gymnastics practice. (Sometimes you might need to do a little creative scheduling to find an hour when you're all free.)

Family Time

Family time is fun time you spend together as an entire family—going to the zoo, playing Crazy Eights, baking strawberry pie, watching a meteor shower, making valentines, hiking in the woods, and so on. Watching *Wheel of Fortune* together does not count. You gotta turn off the boob tube for family time. Sometimes the best communication happens naturally—as organic as bean sprouts—when you're just "being" and everybody is relaxed. When you increase the amount of attention you're paying to each other, the opportunities to talk will also increase. Even if nothing significant is talked about during family time, shared experiences are the building blocks of a strong family unit.

What if talking together is too scary? The Lloyd family had two daughters, ages 9 and 12, and a mom and a dad. They were all private people, uncomfortable with talking about their feelings in public. Unfortunately, they considered the family public, too. Mom and Dad argued only in the privacy of their bedroom. If they misbehaved, Sandra and Alicia were pulled aside and spoken to in soft voices, and dinnertimes—the only time the family spent together—turned miserable if the subject ever got past the neutral, "And how was your day, Dear?" The girls learned early on that the answer should be, "Fine," and that the appropriate answer to the next question, "And what did you do in school?" was, "Nothing." By the time the girls were pushing adolescence, the idea of talking together about family issues made each family member want to scream and run for the woods.

What's the real problem here? It's not that the Lloyds are private—privacy in itself is not a bad thing. I think this family would be happier if they did more activities together. Sharing meals is very important, but this family never does anything together except eat dinner—and *not* talk about their lives. This family needs some family time—shared experiences, giggles, the foundations of trust. Once they've shared a few evenings of fun together, they can add the "heavy" stuff. For this family at this stage in their lives, talking specifically about problems would just feel painful and not much would be accomplished.

ALL IN THE FAMILY

 If you're just starting on this family togetherness thing, don't push it. A relationship—even with your kids—needs time to breathe. Schedule a walk or a bike ride. Take an art class together. Make time to *haaaang*. Once you're not rubbing against each other's rough edges so much, you can begin handling the tougher stuff.

"The Family Will Come to Order"

Family meetings are a focused way to pay attention to the inner workings of your family unit and to help build inner discipline—structure—into your family life. Use regular family meetings to get schedules scheduled, issues hashed out, accomplishments lauded, vacations planned, decisions made and announced, and pizza and popcorn munched. Family meetings are not as casual as family time, but they can be an important aspect of making sure your family life goes smoothly.

Family meetings work best when they're regular (no, no, put away the Metamucil), either once a week or twice a month. And no, they don't have to be a major time commitment. Keep 'em snappy—30 minutes max. Any longer than that and you're going to lose focus and interest. Since *all* family members are active participants in a family meeting, it's best to set up the agenda in advance and let all family members have input. How about a list posted in the kitchen? Everybody can write their concerns and ideas ahead of time, and you can take turns planning the agenda.

When you get to the gnarly issues, hold a *brainstorming session.* Brainstorming works because it involves the whole family, produces lots of ideas in a short time, and encourages creative thinking. Brainstorming also can be done in pairs. Let's say the problem is Bart's constant knuckle-cracking. You're tired of nagging, and Bart is tired of being nagged, tired of being teased at school, and unable to stop. The family holds a brainstorming session. The suggestions below are adapted from William Sonnenschein's book, *The Practical Executive and Workforce Diversity.* Before you start, review these brainstorming rules and procedures:

- Set up a chalkboard, and have one person write down all the ideas generated.

- Think about using turn-taking to get it started, but don't stick to it too long.

- Think of as *many* ideas as possible. Let the juices flow.

- Hold off on judgments—nobody is allowed to say, "That's dumb!" or, "What a terrible idea!" and don't reject any ideas, no matter how stupid-sounding or unfeasible. Often the silliest, most ridiculous, most unfeasible concept leads to a brilliant idea.

- Piggyback—let one idea generate another. Get excited! ("Maybe Bart should wrap a bandage around his hand so he can't crack his knuckles!" "Yeah! Or how about sewing his fingers together!" "Yeah!!")

- Evaluate. Get rid of the unfeasible ideas, "collapse" the similar ideas, and evaluate and prioritize the ones you have left.

- Once the brainstorming is over and a solution decided upon, *write it down.* ("Bart will tie a string to his finger to help him remember not to crack, and *nobody* will say anything if they see him doing it, but they *will* pull at their ear to let him know he's doing it again.")

During your family meetings, *focus on the positive.* It's easy to get carried away with complaints and schedules and forget to acknowledge the great things that happened that week and who was particularly wonderful. Play a game, sing a song, put on the stereo, and have the kids show you "how to dance." Then show *them*. Laugh a lot.

MOM ALWAYS SAID

The hardest part of brainstorming is holding off on judgments until everybody's creative juices are exhausted. Tell that judgmental voice in your head to take a nap or a walk around the block—it's vital.

Just Me and You, Doll Face

Special time is done in duos—one parent and one child. (If you're a single parent with one child, then family time and special time are redundant.) Special time needs to be just that—special. Don't try and confuse the casual conversations you have while you're folding laundry with special time. Special time is supposed to be fun. No chores allowed.

"So, is this when we confront our issues?" Well...maybe. But let's take the word "confront" out of it, okay? When people share pleasant experiences alone together, they start feeling emotionally close. Closeness leads to talking. Sometimes things are best talked about—and discipline is best achieved—in a private setting, one-on-one, mano a mano. But don't ever jeopardize fun during special time (or family time, for that matter). Let any discussions about serious issues grow organically. Don't set them up, and don't *push*. People—and this includes kids—hate to be pushed. Remember that special time is fun time—fun without guilt. Yes, you're being *productive*. Special time pays off in closeness, rapport, and stress reduction. Here are some ideas for special time (maybe they'll generate some ideas of your own):

◆ Take your nine-year-old out for lunch—just the two of you—at regular intervals.

◆ You're both interested in comets, so take an astronomy class with your 11-year-old. Make sure to schedule enough driving time so you can have a leisurely chat in the car.

◆ Spontaneous hot cocoa! You're not sleeping, she's not sleeping, it's late at night. Have a quiet, giggling cocoa party at the kitchen table!

◆ In dire circumstances, you might make an "emergency" special time. Pull off the freeway at a random exit, and watch the wind blow through stray grasses. With a little time and TLC, Tom's gonna confess that he's been stomping around like a bear because the kids at school are teasing him about his jacket.

◆ Go to the movies, but *only* if you schedule time alone afterward to talk about what you saw. If you race to the theater and race on home, you're sorta defeating the purpose. Yes, you'll be together, but you'll be focused on the movie.

If your family members are involved in a lot of different activities outside the house, remember that your kids need time together, too. You'll have to use your imagination about the best way to deliver quality sibling time. A gruesome twosome arts-and-crafts activity? Maybe a class together? Don't give up at the first sign of griping or quarreling. After all, these guys are going to be siblings all their lives. If they haven't spent time together and shared some of the same experiences, how are they going to reminisce about their childhood once you've passed on and they're old, gray, and doddering?

How Much Time *Do* You Share?

Special time is easily compromised, especially when things get nuts. Try noticing how much time you actually spend alone with your child and the quality of attention you give each other during those times. Try this interesting (and sometimes enlightening) exercise: Every day for a week, write down how much actual time you spend alone with your child, what you do or talk about, and what else is going on while you're together. Your list should only reflect the time you spend alone together, not time with all your kids, family time, or time in a group. Provoking guilt isn't my point. It's like that old dieting exercise where you write down every single thing you eat for a week: Awareness is the first step to improvement. When you see clearly what's going on, you're on the path to making change.

REASONABLE MOM, REASONABLE GOALS

Reasonable Mom knows that successes breed success, so when you're thinking about behavior, set your sights on successful goals. Disciplinary goals should be:

- ◆ Specific (not vague and general).

- ◆ Realistic (achievable by your child).

- ◆ Limited in number (don't tackle too many at once).

If your goals are, "I want Robby to obey me, do his chores, and study hard," you risk disappointing yourself and Robby. You may *want* Robby to do all those things, but you're asking a lot. The goals are too vague, so it will be hard for you and Robby to measure his progress. Start by targeting a specific goal you *know* he'll be able to reach, such as, "I want Robby to clean up his room every Saturday." Now you—and Robby—will have a chance at success.

When you're setting up your goals for Robby (or Bobby or Bonny), keep in mind who Robby *is* and how *old* he is. Remember all our talk about appropriate expectations? Time to apply them, Mom. Make sure you're explicit about the goals *with Robby*. Some parents have kids sign little contracts about behavior issues, but I feel this usually isn't necessary. It *is* necessary to make sure that you and Robby know you're talking about the same thing. If Robby thinks cleaning his room means getting the toys off the floor and the dirty laundry into the basket and you think it includes vacuuming and dusting, then you've got a storm a-brewin'.

Family Values (and Standards)

Part of defining your disciplinary goals is understanding your own standards and values, the standards you want your kids to internalize and the values you would like them to learn.

Most parents have a vague sense of their values and how they want their kids to be, believe, and behave, but far fewer have crystallized them into a set of guidelines or rules. Here are two interesting family activities, the first more "serious" than the second, that can tell you a lot about your family's standards and values and help you become more explicit about what you expect.

Developing the Family Rules

Part of establishing limits, family expectations, and disciplinary goals entails figuring out how family members ought to treat each other. You might want to make up a list for all to refer to, sort of like a family mission statement. The family rules state explicitly how the family expects people to behave. This is the bottom line. Some experts recommend posting it on a kitchen bulletin board or on the refrigerator. Developing family rules works best when everybody has some input. Here are some questions to talk about when you're developing your own list:

◆ How do I like people to treat me?

◆ What's the best way to let somebody know how I feel?

◆ Is it okay to hit somebody when I'm angry?

◆ What's the most appropriate way to express anger?

◆ How do I like my things to be treated?

◆ What do I feel are important manners?

◆ When we have a fight, what kind of behavior is okay with me, and what kind of behavior don't I like?

Once you've discussed these issues, start coming up with a list of behavior rules. These should apply to *everybody* in the family— Mom, Dad, kids—everybody except the goldfish and the dog.

In her book, *Positive Parenting from A to Z*, Karen Renshaw Joslin recommends the following four rules:

1. We use words to tell others how we feel. We do not name call or use bad language.

2. We do not hurt others physically or emotionally.

3. We do not hurt each other's property or our own.

4. We work to get out of a problem, not stay in it.

Your rules might be different; make sure there aren't *too* many rules—keep 'em basic.

The Family Motto

The family motto exercise is a fun way to clarify standards and values that you have, but might not often talk about. Grab the whole family impromptu, or schedule it for a family meeting activity. Sit down together with paper, pens, and art supplies, cut some poster paper in the shape of heraldic shields, and make family crests of arms. As you decorate them, talk about what your family motto might be—you might have one, you might have more than one, or you might have one for each member of the family. Here are some examples to get you started:

- The Three Musketeers: All for one, one for all.
- The Olsens: We are not free until we are all free.
- The Flintstones: We rock!

THE LEAST YOU NEED TO KNOW

- Positive discipline is a part of daily life.
- Positive discipline teaches your values, fosters mutual respect, provides positive reinforcement, and uses choices.
- Spending time with your kids is an essential part of teaching positive discipline.
- When teaching discipline, set your sights on successful goals.
- Family rules and mottos are an effective way of setting reasonable expectations for your kids.

5

Talking—and Listening

In This Chapter

◆ Why communication is *so* essential

◆ Learning about talking, learning about listening

◆ Communication strategies for solving problems with your kids

Here's a whole chapter about talking and listening—in one tidy word, *communication!* Communication is Mom's primary disciplinary tool, my fire wall of problem prevention, my first, last, and in-between line of defense, my chicken-soup-for-all-that-ails-ya. Teaching discipline is about talking to your kid in a way she can hear. Hey, if your kid doesn't "get" what you're trying to teach, she's never going to learn. Teaching discipline is about listening to your kid in a way you can understand. Unless you "get" what's really going on in her life, you'll have a hard time raising the reasonable child you want.

TALKING WITH, NOT TO

Nobody likes a lecture, nobody likes to be berated, and nobody learns when they don't like what they're hearing. This includes your kids. So save the stories-with-a-moral for the autobiography.

Here are some general guidelines for talking with instead of to your kids:

◆ Don't lecture, advise, nag, or berate.

◆ Be specific.

◆ Be honest.

◆ Don't let it escalate.

◆ Watch the criticism.

◆ Use "I" statements.

◆ Don't set them up.

Now let's look at these guidelines in more detail.

Don't Lecture, Advise, Nag, or Berate

No self-respecting kid is going to listen to yet *another* lecture on what she should or shouldn't do or be. You're just not going to get anywhere. Even if she doesn't get sassy and say it, she's most likely to turn you off, tune you out, and think, "Who died and made *her* Queen?"

"What? But then how do I correct my kids?" Wow. Uh oh. Do not pass go. Go back to Chapter 4 and review positive discipline.

"But isn't this how most of us talk to our kids?" Yup. And it *is* hard to change. But talking *with* your kids is about creating a dialogue—two people talking together. Talking *to* your kids is merely a monologue—one person talking. You'll know you're monologing when you hear yourself say the naughty words "should" and "have to."

Be Specific

Keep conversations and complaints focused and specific. Don't drag in every crime against humanity your little offspring has ever committed.

Try hard to banish those nasty, nasty words "always" and "never" from your vocabulary. "Amanda, you *never* clean up after yourself!" will do little to solve Amanda's messy habits. Poor Amanda. She'll feel undermined in her efforts (after all, yesterday she *did* hang up her towel after the shower). "Jason, why do you *always* ignore me?" won't help much either. Poor Jason. What if he actually was listening to you this time?

Be specific about what you would like to see. Not, "I expect you to be more responsible," or, "Change your attitude, Kid," but, "I expect you to pick up the towels on the bathroom floor when you're done in there."

Be Honest

You want your kid to be honest? Then gee willikers, Betsy, better tell the truth yourself. Kids have excellent B.S. radar. Honesty includes honesty *to* the kids (yes, you can be reserved—kids don't need to know the gory details) and honesty *in front of* the kids (your kids will emulate you—be a good role model).

Don't Let It Escalate

The point of all this is to get some results, right? When people are yelling, screaming, slamming doors, and crying, the results are likely to be only bad feelings, chipped paint, and neighbors who'll give you the fisheye next time you bump into them at the local gas station. ("Oh, there's *that* mom. My, my, that family sure *fights* a lot.")

Here are some suggestions to prevent the "discussion" from becoming an "argument":

- *Diffuse the tension with laughter.* Warning: This only works if people are not *too* tense. A joke cracked at the wrong time can make things worse. Much worse. And never laugh *at* your kid. That will also make things worse. Much worse.

- *Count to 10—silently.* Count slowly. Then count to 20.

- *Excuse yourself.* You can say, "I'm getting a little worked up here. I'm going to take a brief bathroom break." Splash some cold water on your face.

- *Excuse the child.* "Honey, take five. I'll meet you back in this room at 1:15."

- *Breathe.* When people get really upset, they sometimes forget to breathe, which literally reduces the flow of oxygen to the brain. You *need* your brain, especially when you're upset.

Watch the Criticism

Not all children respond well to verbal criticism. Criticizing behavior can be a negative tactic, and you risk damaging a child's sense of self if you criticize too harshly or too often. Try more positive approaches first—praise and encouragement—and when you do use criticism, make sure he really understands that it's his behavior you're criticizing—it has nothing to do with how much you love him. Keep the criticism very specific, not global. Take thy sword and banish the words "always" and "never" to a far, far kingdom where the sun rarely shines.

Use "I" Statements

Want your side of the story to get some ear-play? Try an "I" statement. When you begin a statement about your perceptions, feelings, or preferences with the word "I," you're more likely to be listened to because you're letting your kid know that you're speaking from your own point of view. (Bonus: Using "I" statements can also help you clarify your own perceptions, feelings, and preferences.)

> **WISE WORDS**
>
> *"I" statements* are statements that, well, begin with the word "I," such as, "I appreciate your coming to dinner when you're called."
>
> "I" statements can help treat *Parent deafness*, an unfortunate syndrome that makes kids with otherwise perfect hearing completely deaf to the wishes or needs of a parental figure.

The statements on the left side of the chart below shut down communication, while the statements on the right side open it up.

CLOSED COMMUNICATION	OPEN COMMUNICATION
"You don't respect me."	"When you talk to me like that, I feel as though you don't respect me."
"Angela, never hit Joanne."	"Wait a minute, we don't hit people in our family. I feel angry when I see that, Angela. Can the two of you please tell me what's going on?"

Using "I" statements implies that you're willing to at least *hear* the other side of the story. Although hitting your sister is never right, maybe Joanne was provoking Angela, in which case Joanne needs to be talked with, too. Saying "Don't hit" ends the conversation. Caput. Done, over with, let's go shopping.

ALL IN THE FAMILY

Some people use a three-part "formula" for "I" statements: 1. when, 2. I feel, and 3. because. Like this: "*When* you stay up very late on a school night *I feel* worried *because* you won't have enough sleep and you'll be tired at school the next day."

When you start a statement with "You," on the other hand, you'll appear to be blaming the kid and seem like you're certain that only your perceptions are correct. (You might well be blaming the kid, but you still wanna be able to talk about it, right?) If you start with a "You" statement and your kid responds with a "You" statement (or vice versa), negative feelings may escalate. Yowza. Check out these two potential scenarios, one using "You" statements and one using "I" statements:

NOT-SO-GREAT SCENARIO	*BETTER SCENARIO*
"You broke my favorite cup!"	"I loved my cup, and I'm really angry that you broke it."
"Well, you shouldn't have left it in the sink!"	"I'm really sorry it broke, Mom. I dumped the frying pan in, and I didn't see it in the sink."
"Well, you...." "Well, *you*...."	"Honey, please try to watch where you're throwing the pots and pans, and I'll try to be better about putting my stuff away."
Tears, anger, recriminations.	Hugs, kisses, resolution.

"I" statements can be practiced anywhere and everywhere! You don't have to announce them—just try and watch the results.

Don't Set Them Up

Hey—play fair! Never try to trick your kid into saying or confessing something, and never force her into a situation where she must lie to save face or protect herself. (For ways to help prevent and deal with lying, check out Chapter 9.) Manipulation and trickery are undermining and show a basic lack of trust in your child (and in your own parenting skills, too). You might get information now, but you'll also get resistance and recriminations later.

LISTEN! (WHAT?)

Listening to your kids is vital to gather information, build strong relationships, show respect, and problem-solve. Kids are smart. They have more sense than people give them credit for, and they're usually pretty savvy about their needs. Listen to your child, and he will help you raise him.

Here's another reason to listen to your kid: Before she'll listen to *you*, she'll want you to listen to *her.* Better give in—whatever you have to say, no matter how well you make your points, it won't help if you're not being heard.

We all have these input devices made out of odd flaps of cartilage on the sides of our heads, otherwise known as ears. They're useful, but they don't do much good if the input sweeps in one ear and whooshes out the other instead of lodging in the brain.

Listening effectively is hard! You might hear something you don't want to hear, or hear something that might challenge your beliefs. You might hear something that will make you want to *change.* As the writer James Baldwin once said, "Most of us are about as eager to be changed as we were to be born, and we go through our changes in a similar state of shock."

Hear Your Kid

Here are some tips for improving your listening skills:

◆ Make a place or time for listening.

◆ Listen at all times.

◆ Try active and proactive listening.

◆ Listen before you leap.

A Time and a Place

Special time—just you and your kid—often presents good listening times. Sometimes an important truth or confidence comes out of silence and the time to let things breathe. Yet sometimes something important will come up just as you're in the middle of a dash to the store, or writing the final notes on your first symphony. Stop for 20 seconds, acknowledge the confidence, and make an appointment to discuss it later. You might say, "Hey buddy, I want to hear more about that. Now's not a good time; I can't pay full attention. How about after dinner tonight at 7:30? Meet you in the living room." Then do it. Kids hate a flaky follow through.

Keep Your Ears Open!

Nah, I'm not contradicting myself—really, I'm not! Remember when Baby was a baby? Even when you were sleeping you kept an ear cocked for a cry. Yeah, your kid is big now, but you should still keep a constant level of awareness. Sometimes things just slip out, or slip into the conversation. Sometimes a child spends all day raising the courage to talk about something, then slips it in at an inconvenient time. If you can, seize the moment. As a parent, you're probably already skilled in the art of rapid prioritizing. What matters most? If Claire is really upset, maybe that letter you're addressing can wait until tomorrow's mail. Set life aside, and listen to your child.

Since kids aren't always completely articulate or even sure about their wants, needs, issues, and opinions—and who of us is?—I sometimes resort to other methods. Active listening and proactive listening are communication techniques that can help you really understand your kid's issues. Actually, they aren't just for moms and their little offspring, they are useful communication tools for *all* relationships.

Active Listening

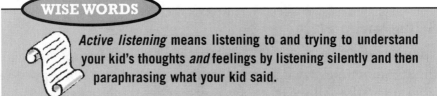

WISE WORDS

Active listening means listening to and trying to understand your kid's thoughts *and* feelings by listening silently and then paraphrasing what your kid said.

Here are the facts and features of active listening:

◆ Active listening can empower your child and raise her senses of self-worth and self-respect. She'll know that you're *really* hearing her when she talks.

◆ Active listening builds empathy. Once you hear your child's concerns, you'll be able to feel a bit of what he's feeling.

◆ Active listening will help you better understand what your kid means. Sometimes kids aren't completely clear (to say the least). Active listening can help.

◆ Active listening gives your kid the opportunity to correct any misunderstandings you might have.

◆ By using active listening, you can prompt your child to explore her thoughts and feelings on a deeper level.

"But Mom, it feels so fake!" Oh, sure, using active listening can seem weird at first. Hang with Mom for a moment, okay? Before you try it for the first time, turn off the TV, stop driving, and focus your attention. Maybe wait until you're having a family meeting or during dinner. Then tell your child what's up—"Hey honey, we're going to play a listening game. You're going to talk, and then I'll tell you exactly what you said. You can tell me if I've got it right, and if you have anything to add, you can add it then."

The older child might be a bit resistant. Oh, that cold-blooded stare! You can try a more informal approach at first by simply listening silently and then paraphrasing *without* calling attention to what you're doing: "So you're saying blah blah blah blah. You feel blah blah blah. Did I get that right?"

When you get more information than you've had in months, when you feel that release in your chest called relief, then you can call me up and say, "Amazing! Mom, this stuff actually works!"

MOM ALWAYS SAID

During the paraphrasing stage of active listening, make sure you're not giving your own interpretations. Simply restate what your child has said. This will help her hear herself, too.

What Can Go Wrong?

Here are some toe-stubbers—impediments to effective active listening:

◆ Hearing what you expect or want to hear.

◆ Allowing your beliefs and attitudes to interfere with your listening. What if your kid tells you about something that goes totally against your values, morals, and belief system? Bite your tongue, Mom. You'll be able to react later. Consider this an information-gathering session, with you as an undercover spy. Your job is to fully understand what your kid is saying.

♦ Allowing your feelings about what's being said to affect how you're listening. Kids push buttons, and man, is it easy to fall into *this* trap. It may take a little practice, but you want to put yourself in active-listening mode and just concentrate on "getting" what's being said. You can react later. Maybe you can have a silent scream–fest in the shower later on.

♦ Paying attention only to how the information is being communicated, not what is actually being said. If Benjamin is slouched over on the couch and mumbling, you might *think* he doesn't care about what he's saying. Try to focus on the content, not the delivery. (Saying, "Sit up straight when you talk to me!" will stop things *cold!*)

♦ Being too literal—not trying to figure out what the child means. Kids sometimes have their own ways of saying things, like the old "bad" meaning "good." If you listen too literally, you're gonna get confused.

♦ Listening only for the facts. How your kid feels about what she's telling you may be just as important. Use your kid's body clues and your own intuition to listen to the entire communication. Then check it with the kid during the paraphrasing part of the exercise.

Proactive Listening

"Ve haf vays of making you talk!" Active listening is about being open and listening without interpretation to your child's perspective. Proactive listening, according to communications expert William Sonnenschein, takes listening a step further. Proactive listening is a "guided" listening technique designed to elicit specific information.

Proactive listening lets you, the listener, be more in control of the communication. Sometimes, as a parent, there is information that you *need* to know, no ifs, ands, or buts—end of discussion. Proactive listening provides a way of getting it without coercion or manipulation, through asking pertinent and probing questions. It's fast and it's subtle, like a jaguar in the jungle. Here are some of the reasons to do proactive listening:

◆ *To get more information.* Your kid may not know what's important. If you're a good proactive listener, you can ask questions to steer the conversation gently over to the important subjects.

◆ *To get deeper into a topic.* He might not understand how much information you want, or he might be trying to keep something from you. Asking the right questions may gain you more information.

◆ *To help your kid clearly express what she's trying to communicate.* You can help her out by directing her with your questions. Here's a bonus: The more she talks about it, the more she may understand her own thoughts and feelings.

Proactive listening is not especially difficult. Ask a question, and listen quietly to the answer. As you listen, find the cues to the areas you feel need to be explored, and ask questions about what has been said. The best proactive listening questions are open-ended—questions that cannot be easily answered with a simple yes or no. *Don't* stop the "exercise" to make judgments or criticize—you'll have lots of time for that later.

Suppose Seth comes home from school complaining that his teacher put him on detention. When you ask, "Well, why did she do that?" Seth mumbles, "I don't know, she just doesn't understand me." If you react, yell, scream, and punish Seth for getting in trouble, you'll probably never find out what's happening with him at school. Instead, you might probe for information: "In what ways doesn't she understand you?" "What happened right before she put you on detention?"

Listen Before You Leap

Listening effectively before reacting is hard; most of us don't have much experience in this matter. Don't expect perfection the first time you try it. It takes years to be a black belt in karate, remember? Practice, practice, practice is the key to becoming a good listener.

PROBLEM SOLVING

I can think of four basic ways to resolve a conflict between parents and children:

1. You can decide what needs to be done. This is the "because I say so" approach. However, if you make a unilateral decision, Junior's gonna be unhappy.

2. Junior can decide what needs to be done. If Junior decides, you're gonna be teed-off.

3. You can compromise. If you compromise, both of you will have to give up a little of what you want in order to come to an agreement. Compromise is okay, but neither of you is likely to be completely satisfied.

4. You can problem-solve. Problem solving may take a little longer, but it's a way for you and your child to collaborate so that both "sides" are happy. In business-speak, they call this a win-win situation. Problem solving uses the talking and listening techniques I've shown you in this chapter.

Problem solving is also a disciplinary technique. It does more than solve an immediate problem, it teaches respect and empathy, helps internalize discipline, and empowers a child by using her as a collaborator on her own problems. Once your child has been through a problem-solving process a couple of times, she'll have a sense of how to think through a problem, apply logic, come up with solutions, and act respectfully and responsibly.

Here's an approach to problem solving using this chapter's techniques. You can problem-solve with your child alone or in a family meeting. Begin your problem-solving session by listening. I've said it before and I'll say it again, kids are smart; if you listen hard enough, they may just give you the answers you, and they, need.

1. *Define the problem.* Use active listening. As you paraphrase what's been said, state her feelings as well as her words and let her correct and amplify. "Elizabeth, you say you hate me

because I like Roger better than I like you. You believe it's not fair that Roger and I went to the movies without you. You're feeling left out, and you want to feel special." Don't jump in with judgment, criticism, analysis, or advice. If you need more information, use proactive listening to dig deeper.

2. *Empathize.* Show you understand the problem and how she feels. You can reminisce a little—"I remember when I was 10 and Grandpa brought Aunt Reva to work with him and I had to stay home. I felt angry and left out, too." But keep it snappy, Mom. You simply want her to know that you really *get* what she's going through.

3. *Express your own feelings about the problem using "I" statements.* Keep blame *way* away from this conversation. "I want to spend special time with each of my children. I love you as much as I love Roger, and I feel sad when you say you hate me." This step will help your child understand your needs— hey, she might start understanding that you *have* needs!

4. *Hold a brainstorming session for solutions* (review the rules in Chapter 4). Got specific ideas you want to add? Stay away from the words and phrases "should," "I would," "I think," and "If you ask me."

5. *After you evaluate the brainstorming ideas, agree on a trial solution.* (Elizabeth and Mom will go swimming during their next special time, something Roger doesn't like to do.) Try not to compromise, give in, or exert your own mighty will. Most problems have a solution. Your creative brainstorming session may very well provide an answer that surprises, and delights, you both.

6. *Once you've decided on a solution, put it into play.* Then follow up! Check back in with your kid after a day or so to see how things are working out. Decide whether you need to give it a little more time (it's hard for kids to be patient) or whether you should begin the problem-solving process again.

THE LEAST YOU NEED TO KNOW

◆ Communication is your primary disciplinary tool.

◆ Nobody likes—or learns from—a lecture. Nix the "I told you so's."

◆ "I" statements are an effective way to open dialogue with your kids and get your feelings and opinions heard.

◆ Active and proactive listening techniques are good skills for the entire family.

◆ Listen to your child, and he will help you raise him.

◆ Problem-solving does more than solve an immediate problem; it teaches respect and empathy.

6

Preventing Problems

It's been a long day. You drift into the kitchen with only one thought on your mind: a delicious midnight snack! But directly across your path, a line of teeming ants wends its way across the floor from the back porch door to the garbage can. Oh! If only you hadn't been so lazy last night! You noticed a couple around 4 A.M. when you got up to get little Sonia a glass of water, but you were so tired. "I'll get those guys in the morning," you thought. But then there was the morning hullabaloo, work, dinner out, and now… ANT INVASION!!!!!! It's so much harder to deal with now that it's a problem.

Sometimes, alas, raising kids feels like this.

Let the clichés fly: An apple a day keeps the doctor away. An ounce of prevention is worth a pound of cure. This is a chapter about preventing behavior problems. In previous chapters, I talked about fostering mutual respect and good communication. This chapter focuses on positive reinforcement, limits, and choices, with a few other "apples a day" and "ounces of prevention" in between.

It's much easier—and far more pleasant—to deal with a couple of stray ants than it is to have to spray 'n' wipe a thick column of them. And it's far easier to *prevent* behavior problems in kids than it is to deal with the problems once they're full-blown. Remember the art of paying attention? Preventing discipline problems is about paying attention to what's going on in the little hearts and minds of your offspring and nipping problems in the bud *before* they begin.

Whoa! If you're having problems with your kid, don't do anything itchy or rash like skipping this chapter. These techniques work to help fix existing problems, too.

POSITIVE REINFORCEMENT

Positive reinforcement should occur every single day. Using positive reinforcement—encouragement, descriptive praise, and rewards—does two primary things. It helps increase the frequency of positive behavior in our children, and it helps our kids see—and understand the value of—their own positive qualities and actions.

Granted, not everything your child does is great; if you pretend it is, you're doing your child a disservice. Yet providing positive reinforcement is *not* just cheerleading. You're *not* going to turn into pretty Pollyanna, seeing only the silver linings in ugly storm clouds. No, this is a reality-based, sound parenting technique that can help turn your child's behavior around—often *very* quickly. Give it a shot.

> **WISE WORDS**
>
> *Positive reinforcement* means supporting your child's positive deeds and qualities through enthusiasm, encouragement, specific praise, and rewards. It reinforces what the child is doing right, rather than concentrating on what she's doing wrong.

Facing the Facts

Here are some questions you will want to ask yourself as you begin thinking about positive reinforcement:

- How often do you criticize your child?

- How often do you provide specific, positive feedback?

- In what ways do you show your pride, enthusiasm, and confidence in him?

James Windell, author of *8 Weeks to a Well-Behaved Child,* suggests making a week-long tally of every time you make a critical remark or negative statement to your children. During that week, watch for excessive anger and disappointment (we're usually most critical when we're angry). Don't try to change your normal behavior, just make notes. At the end of the week, add up your tally. You may be pleasantly surprised; you may be appalled. Either way, it's *only* a starting place. Mom's Motto #14: Knowledge is necessary (even when it hurts).

Most parents, when they really analyze their behavior, find that they parent their children far more through criticism than they do through focusing on the good stuff. It's easy to notice the stuff that annoys. It's harder to comment on what works. Some parents are so frightened of spoiling their children that they *never* provide positive reinforcement. I find that sad, and wrong.

Windell also suggests making a list of 5 or 10 things you really like about your kid—the assets of talent, skill, and temperament she will be able to call on throughout her life. This exercise will help you refocus your attention on what's truly important about your child.

Making lists of good qualities—of others and of yourself—can also be useful when you're *really* angry. It can calm you down and help put things in perspective. Pretty soon, you're ready to begin problem solving.

Using Encouragement and Descriptive Praise

Children will live up to your expectations. Tell them they're no-good snakes in the grass and they'll get down on their bellies and start crawling. Assume they will do their best, and reward them with words and encouragement, and you'll have the kind of kids you want. Encouragement is vital.

Comment on specific, wonderful things your child is doing, such as a kindness to a friend. Comment when you see improvement, such as not complaining about math homework. Comment when you see effort, such as emptying the dishwasher without being asked. The more specific your encouragement, the more a kid will learn to figure out for himself when he's doing a good job.

If you're going to use praise, make it descriptive. For instance, rather than saying, "You painted a great picture, Ellen," say, "I like the yellow dog in the corner. And what an interesting choice of color for that tree!" *Descriptive praise* encourages the child. Non-descriptive praise teaches a child to please others.

Descriptive praise is a form of encouragement that describes what you like about a child's actions. It uses specific commentary rather than generalities.

I mean *real* praise and *real* encouragement. No faking, Mom! Kids are smart; they know when they've done well, and they know when they aren't performing up to snuff. If you tell a kid what a great athlete he's becoming when he *knows* he's the worst in the class, you'll break your trust by lying to him. Focus on the positive—his improvement, his attitude, his willingness to try and fail—but don't *lie*.

Rewards and Bribes

A lot of child development experts recommend rewards over bribes. Why? What's the difference? As I see it, the difference between rewards and bribes is the difference between training and education.

A reward happens after the fact, in return for a kid doing the best she can. A rewarded child learns, "When I do well, I'm appreciated and rewarded." A reward might be used like this: "Amy, I really appreciate how you listened to instructions when you worked with Uncle Frank on the car today. I think we should all go out for ice cream to celebrate."

A bribe is promised in advance as a motivator. Bribery is a bit too much like dog training, in my book. "Sit boy, good doggy, yes, here's your treat." "If you do your homework, I'll take you out for ice cream." See the similarity? Bribes are often used in conjunction with threats: "If you *aren't* rude to your sister while Grandma is here, you can stay up late and watch *Xena*. If you *are* rude, no *Xena* for you, and you can pretty much forget about that new watch you've been asking for."

> ### WISE WORDS
>
> A *reward* is something nice offered in response to positive behavior.
>
> A *bribe* is something promised in advance to try and bring about positive behavior.

What do you want your kids to achieve? Do you want Jo to be nice to Amy because she wants to watch TV and get a new watch? Or do you want her to be nice to Amy because she's her loving sister and she's not interested in making Grandma uncomfortable?

"Oh, right," you say, rolling your eyes and throwing this book against the wall in disgust. "That's all very well, Mom, but you haven't met *my* kid. She's not going to do anything nice unless she's coerced or threatened—maybe not even then." Go pick up the book. I hope you didn't bend it! Most parents resort to the occasional bribe. I'm not a purist, and I'm not against the occasional motivation by bribery. Sometimes you just need results. Just keep in mind that bribery works *best* when it's used very occasionally.

Chores

Yes, chores can be a form of problem prevention, too. Hang on, Mom hasn't flipped her lid. Here's the equation: Chores provide a way for a child to learn to take responsibility. Kids who are given responsibility, who contribute to family life, and who feel their contributions are valued have an increased sense of self-worth.

And a kid with a strong sense of self-worth is less likely to engage in "problem" behavior.

CHOICES

Door #1 or Door #2? Sugar or bananas in the cereal? Left or right at the light? Love or money? High school dropout or Ph.D. program? The red shirt or the blue shirt? It's important that your children understand they have choices in life, and it's vital that they learn how to make them.

"As long as you're under my roof, I make the decisions here," says Authoritarian Audrey. Actually, Audrey is deluding herself. She has influence, but no control. Her kids do have choices, and there's nothing she can do about it.

Audrey needs to do three things:

1. *Give it up and admit that kids have choice.* When they're little, yeah, she can restrict their choices. But older kids *always* have a choice in the matter, since, whatever the matter is, they can always choose noncompliance. (For some kids, noncompliance is the *only* choice, which is why you have rebellion.)

2. *Admit that choice is a* good *thing.* Allowing a child to make choices helps prevent problems by empowering the child. An empowered child is a Reasonable Child. Choice-making also helps teach internal discipline. As kids learn the process of consciously choosing, they also learn they have some power and control over their futures.

3. *Learn how to work* with *choice.* When choices and the choice-making process are made explicit, there's less room for misunderstandings to occur. Fewer misunderstandings means more peace in the family. Hoorah! Hoorah! Sis boom bah!

You have three ways of providing choice:

1. *You can provide choices explicitly—providing your child with limited choices.* This is similar to the way you used to treat your kid when she was four: "Which shirt do you want to wear, the striped or the flannel?"

2. *You can give your child the responsibility of making choices that lead up to a desired event.* For example, you can say, "You need to do your homework, call Grandpa to thank him for his card, and be in bed by 9:30 tonight. It's up to you how you arrange to do that."

3. *You can point out a choice your child is making and what consequences are attached to that choice.* If the deal is that homework must be done before any TV is watched, you might say, "I see that you're choosing not to watch TV tonight." Does this sound snotty? It doesn't have to be. Some kids need a little more experience realizing what consequences their actions are provoking.

MOM KNOWS BEST

Eleven-to-thirteens can be a little like four-year-olds—"big kids" one moment, "babies" the next. If too many choices overwhelm your adolescent, limits can help: "Tuna or salami?"

EFFECTIVE, REASONABLE LIMITS

In Chapter 2, I stressed the importance of providing reasonable limits for your kids. Here are a few hints about the "how" of it.

Before you decide on a limit, it's gotta pass the "limit test":

◆ Review your family rules (in Chapter 4). Does the limit fit within your value system?

◆ Is it a limit for the sake of having some limits? Sometimes overeager parents start going wild with the limit-setting. Cool out. You don't need to discipline for the sake of discipline.

Don't leap to no. Listen to yourself talk. Do you really mean it? No means no. Joan's first impulse when her son Paul made a request was to say no. "Why not?" he'd ask. Silence, while Joan would try to figure out why, indeed, not. Sometimes (after some whining by Paul or a pause for reflection by Joan) she would realize that she had no clear reason or was being too stringent, then she'd have to back down.

What if you don't know an answer? Sometimes you need to confer with a parenting partner. (I'll have a whole section about this in Chapter 10.) Sometimes you may need to think about it. Think twice. Think 10 times. You can take a few minutes—or a few hours—to decide. Rarely do you need to make a decision *so* fast that you can't take time to think it through. Getting pressure? Try saying, "I'm not sure how I feel about that. I need some time to think about it." Or, you can ask your child to tell you why she wants to do something.

"We'll See"? What Does That Mean?

Some parents can be easily typed. When they say, "We'll see," the kids can lay odds that the answer will eventually be no. Is this you? Is the answer "We'll see" leaping from your lips because you don't feel comfortable asserting yourself and need some time to gain courage?

Other parents can be typed the other way. Their "We'll see" is so predictably a yes that the Swiss could run their trains by it. See yourself in this picture? You don't have to be tough—just firm.

Look, I know it takes energy to set limits, but the pay-off is worth it. Once your kid really *gets* that no is no, you'll see a steep drop in the number of pleeeaazes and whine-nots.

Once You Decide to Set a Limit

Once you decide to provide a limit, state it with a clear voice, as though you're presenting a rule of nature, the same way you would say, "The sky is above us." Try it now: "You can listen to music until 8:00 and then the CD player goes off." Try another one: "You may have one more cookie, and that's it." Hear the new authority in your voice?

MOM KNOWS BEST

"My decision is final." It's hard to say those words and *mean* them. Make your voice goes down at the end of the sentence: "No. My decision is fin$_{al}$." Try it.

Reinforcing the Limits

When things get exciting and life begins moving swiftly, it's easy for kids of all ages to forget their rules and limits. For instance, you might remind Anton, who's allergic to wheat, that he shouldn't have pizza at the party. Or ask Sarah, "Hey, remember what you're going to say if Nancy wants you to bug her brother?" Reminders are not the same as nagging (though your kid might accuse you of that—"I know, Mom!"). Reminders simply—and clearly—bring the rule or limit to the front of the brain where your child is more likely to remember it. Repetition is a vital part of learning.

Look, there's bound to be some backsliding. Don't hate yourself; don't hate your kid. Changing behavior patterns takes time. People need to do something many times before it becomes a habit. Somebody once told me—as she struggled to kick a nasty nicotine addiction—that it takes 20 repetitions for something to sink in. And that goes for *you*, too.

Flexibility Is Strength

Did you ever study a language? Sometimes the exceptions to the rules of grammar take more time to learn than the rules themselves. That's not what you're aiming for, but life and parenting are never predictable, and flexibility is one of the greatest strengths you can build in yourself. Firmness is not the same as rigidity. Don't enforce limits just 'cause you said it was a limit; you may need to reevaluate or provide exceptions in cases of need.

But don't do it by default or just because you don't want to assert yourself. I said in cases of *need!* It's like speeding in a car: If it's 4 A.M., the streets are deserted, and you're driving a heart attack victim to the emergency room, you might need to exceed the 25 mph speed limit. Before you *do* change your mind, put it through the "limit changing" test. There are two areas where limits are non-negotiable, non-compromisable, sorry, no way, Bub:

◆ Is it a question of values?

◆ Is it a question of safety?

Changing the Limits

Many (though not all) limits are meant to be stretched and exceeded as a child grows. Keep evaluating, keep in touch with your child's development, and keep on talking. If you're having difficulty figuring out "age appropriate" limits or suspect that your kid has outgrown current limits:

◆ *Check out what your kid's peers' limits are.* Hold it! This is not vindicating all the times Melanie said, "But all the *other* kids...." You're just gathering information.

◆ *Visit your local public library or bookstore and check out the parenting shelves.* You'll find rows and rows of books on child development. Some of them are excellent.

◆ *Talk with your child's teacher.* This is another "involved" adult who sees your child in a very different way than you do and who might have a whole new perspective. Don't wait for parent-teacher conferences. Make your own appointment. Josephine doesn't need to be in trouble for you to get to school.

◆ *Talk with your kid.* If she is "vested" in making decisions about her own limits, she's more likely to live within them without too much chaffing at the bit.

OTHER PREVENTION TECHNIQUES

Here's a technique for preventing "minor" problems: Ignore them! I don't mean that you should turn your back and whistle a happy tune while your kid hauls off and hits the neighbor kid or spends her afternoon tearing wings off butterflies. But sometimes your kid will enter "testing mode" and try some "bad" behaviors just to see what will happen or to get your goat. Rudeness is a very common example of this. Sometimes the best response is no response. This is harder than it seems—can *you* ignore food being drooled out of the mouth?

Ignoring can help keep isolated instances of behavior from becoming chronic problems. If you start the old nag-a-roo when your kid has done something once, you may be in for it.

Ignoring negative behavior is more than just "not encouraging." It's part of the shift from negative to positive parenting, from being your child's opponent to being her ally. As much as possible, notice the good and refrain from criticizing.

MOM ALWAYS SAID

Ignoring behavior doesn't mean lying about your reactions. When you express honest disappointment and anger in a fair way, you're showing respect for your child.

Remove Temptation

The spirit may be willing, but the flesh is too often all too weak. Why test your child? If your kid is not allowed to watch TV except on weekends, don't leave the TV in his bedroom. Don't say, "No sweets or soft drinks," and then stock the cupboards full of 'em. Plan for success, not failure.

"I Respectfully Request..."

If you want something done, ask! A child—hey, any person—will often respond better to a request than a command. Try asking first. "John, will you please hang up your jacket?" Say John doesn't hang up his jacket. At that point, you can say, "I asked you nicely to hang up your jacket. Now I'm not asking. Hang it up now, please."

Remember, kids model their behavior on yours. A child who learns to request what he wants or needs clearly will do better socially than Bossy Billy who orders people around all the time.

FINDING THE BALANCE

Preventative medicine is still medicine, and it doesn't always taste so yummy. Your kids may give you a little grief. Plunging rapidly—tomorrow—into a completely new behavior mode is not a great idea. You'll all be reeling from the shock. Take it slow, one toe into the cold water at a time. You'll soon find out how refreshing it is.

Here are a few more notes about preventing problems:

♦ *Take time out for parents!* Cool down. Count to 417.

♦ *Try tackling one problem at a time.* Behavior problems are often linked, though the links may not be all that clear. Sometimes, when one problem is corrected, a lot of other problems correct themselves, too!

♦ *Work within your parenting style.* Sometimes parents say, "You know, your advice seems sound, but I can't talk to my kid like that, it sounds so *fake!*" Hey, I'm not trying to script your life. Everybody has a different style of being in this world. Some people are outgoing. Some are clear and assertive about what they want and need. Some people are quiet. Some are shy. Some have a harder time expressing emotions. Some yell, some whisper, some laugh a lot, and some are more serious. There's room for positive discipline within every parenting style.

THE LEAST YOU NEED TO KNOW

♦ It's easier to *prevent* behavior problems in kids than it is to deal with the problems once they're full-blown.

♦ Positive reinforcement is strong preventative medicine.

♦ It's important that your kids understand they have choices in life, and it's vital that they learn how to make them.

♦ When providing limits, don't leap to no.

♦ Positive discipline can exist within any parenting style.

What's the Problem Here? (And Whatcha Gonna Do About It?)

You've talked, you've listened, you've problem-solved, you've set family guidelines, and you spend special time together. You have a weekly family meeting. In general, you believe that you're a responsible, respectful Reasonable Mom. Life is good, and you're even better! But then, whoops, the little pip-squeak does something wrong!

"Arghhhh! Where's my belt!"

No, no. Down, girl. Good doggie. It happens. These are kids we're talking about, not robots. Kids test, misbehave, and exasperate. It's part of their job description.

But how *are* you going to respond? To find the most appropriate action—or consequence—to fit a misbehavior, you first must understand the misbehavior and the problem behind it. Is this random misbehavior, a cry for help, a moment of thoughtlessness, trifling naughtiness, or symptoms of serious misbehavior? Okay, Detective Mom, don the trench coat. Time to do some investigating. This chapter focuses on understanding what's *really* going on.

HOW DO I REACT?!

Oh no! Billy has been a bad boy. Perhaps it's minor—chores didn't get done after hours of nagging and promises. Maybe it's moderate—you get a dreaded call from the principal's office. Or you come into the house and face the evidence of an ugly misdeed. Let's say it's really bad—police officers are involved. Take a deep breath. What's your first impulse? Probably a small feeling of panic and the sense that you need to "teach him a lesson." That you need to simply stop the behavior and prevent it from happening ever again.

Here's Mom's advice: No matter *what* you do, you *won't* be able to prevent it from ever happening again. You just don't have that much control over your child! Face it: You are not in control. You have influence, but ultimately no control. If you can understand that—it's a hard one to get—you're halfway there.

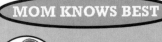
MOM KNOWS BEST

Mom's Motto #744: Don't *react, respond.*

Using—Not Abusing—Your Anger

Anger is good, when used correctly. Anger is a strong emotion closely related to passion. Everybody gets angry, teed-off, pissed, annoyed, furious, and irate. The trick is to use your anger to effectively teach discipline while improving your relationship with your child.

All parents "lose their cool" sometimes. Hey, this is not always a bad thing! It shows your child that you're not the infallible goddess you normally appear to be (hah!), and it shows her that angry feelings *can* be expressed in ways that are not hurtful. Getting angry is human. Problem-solving your way out of conflict and anger is an important lesson to learn.

Here are some quick tips for managing and directing your anger in a positive way:

◆ Use your anger to express your expectations, emotions, values, and needs in a helpful way. Stating to your child clearly what you're angry about, and what you expect your child to do about it, shows your child how strongly you feel about her and her behavior. Using "I" statements (see Chapter 5) will help.

◆ Take a cool-down break. Leave the room, count to 10, and go pound a pillow in another room.

◆ Don't be a chicken and take your pecking-order anger out on your kid. Direct your anger to your boss, or vent it on a friend. Don't let it leak over onto your child. Warn him that you're a grump, reassure him that you're not pissed off at him, and maybe even explain briefly—no need for details— what's making you angry.

◆ Never threaten violence out loud. It's okay to want to break a child's neck, and it might help you relieve some tension by thinking that thought (it's normal, in fact), but it can frighten and threaten a child to say those violent thoughts out loud.

◆ Still angry after the situation is resolved? Don't bottle it up, 'cause it's gonna blow! Vent on somebody, walk it off, or shout it into the wind. Expressing angry feelings helps relieve them.

◆ Breathe, baby, breathe.

Overreacting

In this society, moms expect a lot from their children and even more from themselves. While having high expectations and standards for kids is a good thing, it's easily overdone. Women especially hold themselves to an ideal: the perfect mother, the perfect house, the hardest worker. Women are taught to be "nice," to please others first, and somehow, without complaining too much, to get it all done—dishes, ironing, art projects, car pool, business report, back rub, and garden. Society says that moms need to look good doing it, too.

When moms hold themselves to this level of perfection, they usually hold their kids to those standards, too. Everything is scheduled so tightly that there's no room for the messiness of living.

When so much is at stake, when it feels as though the very success of being a modern woman is hinging on things running smoothly, a child's misbehavior can cause an *extreme* overreaction. You can feel as though your child is letting you down. It's only natural. It's also something to work on.

Your kid is not you. Don't take her behavior personally. Take care of yourself; spend a little time every day doing something *just for you*. Turn on a CD and dance wildly for six minutes. Eat a ripe peach. Read a short story. These little "replenishments" are not self-indulgent; they are a necessary part of parenting. In order to figure out why your child is misbehaving and what to do about it, you need to have some distance from the situation. To gain distance, you need to separate yourself from your child.

While you do need to take responsibility for your actions, you do not need to claim blame.

WHAT'S THE REAL PROBLEM HERE?

Okay, you've gotten angry and reacted, you've cooled down a bit, and now you can work on your response. Deal with the problem.

So what's *really* going on? Ah, if life were only like a book, spelled out clearly in black and white! immutable and unchanging! Children—like life—are not simple and easy to read. They very often say, do, and act a certain way, while inside they feel just the opposite.

Let's get clear on this: The problem is not *who* the kid is, it's *what* she's doing. A child wants to please. Separate the deed from the doer. Take a leap of faith. The kid who has misbehaved feels bad about it, at least at some level.

Jeanne Elium and Don Elium, authors of *Raising a Son, Raising a Daughter,* and *Raising a Family,* teach parents to look for the *positive intent.* They say there is always an underlying meaning—a positive intent—to our words and actions. Looking for this positive intent can help ease your own frustration and solve the problem at hand.

> **WISE WORDS**
>
> *Looking for the positive intent* is the practice of finding good intentions beneath a person's words and actions, no matter what the result.

Here are two examples of looking for positive intent to understand the problem:

◆ Nine-year-old Corinne was supposed to call immediately after school if she wanted to play at her friend Eliza's house. One afternoon, she finally showed up at 6:30 P.M. to face a couple of terrified and angry parents. What was Corinne's positive intent? Corinne wanted to grow up and take on more independence.

◆ Twelve-year-old Paul flushed his report card down the toilet, unfortunately clogging up the plumbing and causing a whole lot o' plumbers' fees! We could make a snap judgment and say that Paul is obviously a juvenile delinquent who will be doing hard time in the Big Hokey within a couple of years. Or, we could look for the positive intent. Paul's report card showed a D in math, and he was afraid of his parents' reaction and ashamed of disappointing them. Looked at that way, the response to Paul's action can encompass more than punishment. Maybe his parents will examine their own expectations. Maybe Paul will get some tutoring—and some counseling.

RELATED, RESPECTFUL, AND REASONABLE

When it's time to select a response and a consequence to misbehavior, the first thing to think about is what you want the consequence to achieve. Remember that the point of discipline is to teach your child internal control over her behavior. You're training the voice of consequence that will speak in her head for the rest of her life before she takes an action. When she's 33 and boldly living a life far away from you ("Waaahhh!" Oh, calm down, she'll still call you every weekend!) that voice shouldn't be saying, "If you miss this deadline, you can't eat chocolate cake for a week." It should be saying, "If you miss this deadline, your boss will be let down, and you may not get the raise you were expecting."

Natural and Logical Consequences

Back in Chapter 2, I talked briefly about "natural" and "logical" consequences. While not all consequences will work with all kids, the most effective consequences are often logical extensions of natural consequences. Kids have a strong sense of fairness and respond well when they feel a consequence is naturally related. Natural consequences help you avoid power struggles because they're a direct extension of an action, not something totally arbitrary imposed by you, the all-powerful, all-controlling mom.

Say, for example, you feel that Sue, age 12, should not wear miniskirts to school unless she's wearing opaque stockings. You've talked about your reasons for the limit, and Sue agrees that wearing highly revealing clothing isn't appropriate for school. Then you see her on the corner, brazen bare legs and all. This is clearly a violation of the limits. *Inappropriate* responses and consequences might include: calling her a slut, telling her she'll come to a bad end, denying her piano lessons, or grounding her for disobeying.

Once you calm down and consider her positive intent (wanting to fit in with the other kids, enjoying her brand-new attractiveness to boys), you can impose some natural and logical *appropriate* consequences. These might range from expressing your disapproval and letting her know there will be more serious consequences if she does it again to (if this has happened more than once or is part of a pattern) taking away her clothing allowance or insisting that you go with her when she shops for clothes.

MOM ALWAYS SAID

Dump the "I'll show her" mentality. "If you think I'm taking you shopping after the way you..." isn't going to work. You need to be clear about consequences *before* the misbehavior gets out of hand.

Keep consequences explicit! When possible, define them ahead of time. (This forces you to think about them, right?) When applying consequences, always state what and why. And please, Mom, resist the temptation to be vindictive when things go wrong. If you find yourself staring at a sulky child at the dinner table and saying, "If you think I'm going to give you dessert after the way you treated your brother today, think again, Young Man!" you've probably not been explicit enough about consequences.

Keep Consequences Reasonable

Part of determining what's reasonable is trying to keep a sense of perspective about things. Say you and Marty, age nine, are sitting next to each other at the dinner table. Marty is restless, and he keeps kicking your leg. You ask him nicely to stop. A few minutes later, it happens again. You grit your teeth and try to ignore it. By the fifth time Marty kicks you, you've had it! Your blood pressure rises, your urge to kill sets in, and you turn and scream, "Get down now and go to your room! I don't want to see you back here until you can sit like a reasonable person. And absolutely no dessert for you for the next week! You piss me off! You're always bugging me like that. That's not how I raised you!"

Whoa, Mom. Anger is a reasonable reaction to irritation, but the action resulting from your anger was not. Obviously, Marty's "crime"—that of being a restless nine-year-old—is not that great, at least when compared to vandalism, murder, or even destroying his sister's dollhouse by using it as a trampoline.

Establish a scale in your mind with the bottom being "minor irritants" and the top being "calamitous world events." As you react—and then respond—to misbehaviors, stick your child's behavior on the scale. Try to keep things in perspective.

Keep Responses Respectful

And, of course, responses and consequences should be respectful of the child, of her individuality, of her body, of her person as a whole. Take care of your kid. "Okay, don't brush your teeth, you'll see what you'll get. Cavities!" is a natural consequence that is not respectful of your child's body.

When kids mess up, remember the concept of positive intent. Respect the fact that they have good intentions.

MOM KNOWS BEST

It's been said that the road to hell is paved with good intentions. So, I'll contend, is the road to heaven.

Follow Through

If you say you're going to do it, follow through! If you stick to your decisions and are confident in your responses, your kids will respect and trust you for it. Remember that they're relying on you to be firm; they don't yet know how to be.

Being Flexible and Letting Go

Following through on a decision doesn't mean beating a dead horse, or refusing to admit it when you've made a mistake. Au contraire, ma mère! Sometimes, a response or consequence isn't right. Other times, no matter what you do, it doesn't work. These are the times to be flexible. Part of being flexible is being prepared to give up. Sometimes when you retreat from battle, your kid realizes he was fighting for the sake of fighting and relents.

THE STORY OF SNARLING NORA

Here's a case study that illustrates my approach to analyzing the "inner truth" of a situation, while focusing on the positive.

One day, out of the blue, you walk into 11-year-old Nora's room, and she turns to you and screams, "I hate your guts, you fat, ugly moron!" Ouch! Her words sting like a hornet bite. Inwardly, you reel. What do you say? What do you do?

The first thing that occurs is your *reaction* (I'll talk about your *action* later).

Here are some possible reactions:

◆ *You yell back, "How dare you speak to me like that, young lady!"*
You certainly shouldn't have to put up with abuse, but by yelling at Nora, you get in the way of finding out why she's acting the way she is. Same with saying, "What's gotten INTO you?" Nora is not likely to give you a straight or communicative response if you respond like this, no matter how natural your response might be.

◆ *You haul off and belt her one.* Yikes. This gives Nora the message, "You have no right to be angry with me, and if you express your anger in an unacceptable and cruel way, I'll be cruel right back and show you that I'm more powerful than you are." Things will escalate. Keep in mind that it's a normal reaction to *want* to haul off and belt Nora, or at least yell back at her. Resist your impulses—hitting her will only make things worse. I'll get more into the case against corporal punishment in Chapter 8.

◆ *You cry.* This is an honest response. As a first response, there's nothing wrong with it. It shows Nora that she's being heard, that, yes, she does have some effect on you, and that you were injured by her mean words. You will need to follow up on her obvious anger and your response to it. Ask yourself: Am I crying because my feelings were hurt? Or, am I crying because I raised such a terrible daughter who would say such mean things to me? Beware of using guilt as a way to keep Nora in line. We'll talk more about guilt in the next chapter.

◆ *You cool out, regroup, and try to translate.* You take deep breaths and say, "Nora, I feel very upset by what you just said and I'm going to leave the room for a minute to calm down. I'll talk with you in 10 minutes in the kitchen." Yes, of course this is the *ideal* way of reacting. Don't beat yourself up if you didn't manage it this time. Change takes time.

After the Storm

Nora will join you in the kitchen in 10 minutes. In the meantime, you're trying to calm down. "Oh, why?" you moan. "What did I do to deserve this?" It's easy to jump to: "She's doing this to punish me," or, "She said that because she's a no-good little imp. She's cruel, rude, and discompassionate."

Forget for a moment the words she used. Nora was expressing anger and frustration. By saying, "I hate your guts, you fat, ugly moron!" she was using words she knew would slice through you. Now is the time for you to put the words aside and think about the underlying problem.

Okay, Detective Mom, ask yourself the question, "What's the real problem here?" Nora is spewing negativity for a reason. If you can figure out that reason, you'll be far more able to help her—and your relationship.

There are a few questions to be asked here:

◆ What was going on when Nora lost it and got abusive?

◆ What's been happening recently, with Nora and with you?

◆ What was Nora's positive intent?

◆ What are Nora's needs?

◆ What are your needs? (What are you going to do to make yourself feel better for the crummy, cruel, and despicable way she has just treated you?)

Try, try, try to separate these things out.

MOM KNOWS BEST

"Are you asking for a spanking, young lady?" Of course not. What *is* she asking for? Attention? Affection? Independence? Nurturing? Limits? Privacy? Respect? Responsibility?

What's Going On?

You walked into Nora's room. Did you knock? No, the door was open. Maybe Nora needed privacy and had forgotten to shut the door. In that case, perhaps some of her anger was self-directed. Just *who* was she calling the fat, ugly moron? Kids, especially 11-year-olds, increasingly need a sense of privacy in their lives. At the same time, they don't always know *what* they want or *how* to achieve it.

Think about what's been going on in Nora's life. How do her relationships with her friends seem to be going? What about her schoolwork? Have there been any sudden changes in her behavior? (If her grades have taken a nosedive, if she's sleeping a lot, if her grooming habits have gotten worse—a lot worse—you may be dealing with larger issues than normal 11-year-old angst. Check out Chapters 11, 12, and 13.)

Are You Getting Along?

Besides all the nasty, difficult behavior that can be attributed to her being 11, and thus a beast (though a sweet one!), how *have* things been going between you? Do you know why Nora is so angry? Have you been communicating well? (Oh yeah, she's 11. Chances are you're not communicating all that well.)

Before you react or rush to judgment, STOP and think about whether the behavior you're seeing is "developmentally appropriate." Think about it this way: It's all right—even appropriate—for a one-year-old to fling his food on the floor. This behavior is *not* appropriate for an eight-year-old. It's not "abnormal" (though it's worrisome) for an 11-year-old to experiment with shoplifting; it's *never* "normal" for him to experiment with bank robbery.

ALL IN THE FAMILY

Stealing is not necessarily a sign of delinquent behavior. In preteens and teens it's usually a by-product of phase-related issues: peer pressure, rebellion, and so on. Developmentally, stealing is the most "normal" between the ages of five and eight.

The Talk

Nora, sullen, has arrived in the kitchen. It's time to check in with her. Review Chapter 5 for hints about talking with and listening to her. Begin the conversation with some "I" statements, then do some active and proactive listening.

As you listen, it becomes evident that Nora's positive intent was to communicate, "I'm feeling angry, and I feel like you're not seeing or hearing me!" Her, "I hate your guts, you fat, ugly moron!" can be translated as, "I need attention!" and also as, "I need to be left alone." Nora is growing up. She needs more privacy, and she's trying to separate from you. She needs some acknowledgment of this fact. Her conflicting emotions terrify her, and she could use some help getting it all sorted out.

Taking Care of Yourself

Understanding Nora doesn't mean you grant her the right to treat you like mud on the bottom of her delicate foot. Yet, once you see what her needs are, her attack doesn't feel quite as random or shocking. You've let her know that you disapprove of the way she "spoke" to you. The hug she lets you give her at the end of your talk makes you feel better. You resolve to give her more "space," but to watch closely for those times when she needs attention.

This incident was resolved without resorting to additional disciplinary consequences. In the next chapter, I'll focus on techniques to use at times when you—and your child—don't get off so easily!

THE LEAST YOU NEED TO KNOW

◆ Before you figure out what to do about a misbehavior, it's important to understand what caused the misbehavior.

◆ Try to get through your initial reaction to misbehavior before you formulate your response.

◆ Keep consequences explicit, reasonable, and respectful.

◆ When your child is misbehaving and you're feeling unhappy about it, remember to take care of yourself, too.

What Will, Might, and Won't Work

This is a "toolbox" chapter, for use when positive reinforcement, consistency, and limits just aren't quite enough. There are many disciplinary theories and techniques out there: some good, some not so good, and some downright cruel. In this chapter, I'll discuss a variety of appropriate, iffy, and inappropriate disciplinary techniques and consequences. Here are the pros, and here are the cons. Ladies (and gentlemen), choose your weapons...er...*tools*.

WHAT'S IN MOM'S TOOLBOX?

No technique works all the time, or with all kids, and no technique works if used incorrectly or at the wrong time. No matter how hard you try, you're going to make mistakes. No parent is perfect; no parent should try to be. The most important aspect of parenting is love.

Love and paying attention.

And while you're busy paying attention, here are some disciplinary ideas and discussions of their effectiveness. You may need to use a combination of techniques, or you may need to come up with your own. The key is flexibility. (Come to think of it, isn't flexibility the key to life? I'll make that Mom's Motto #482.)

MOM ALWAYS SAID

If you've used negative or ineffective disciplinary methods in the past, there is *no* need to beat yourself up about it! Guilt does no good. It's *never* too late to start using positive methods.

Talk About It/Stop Talking About It

In most cases, talking is the first and best response to behavior problems. Keeping communication lines open is the primary positive disciplinary tool, and often talking is all that's needed to change behavior, or to make sure that it doesn't happen again. You can use the talking and listening techniques discussed in Chapter 5.

Sometimes, however, you *don't* want to talk about it. Certain behavior is simply unacceptable and everybody knows it—you, your kid, and the neighbors. Or, you may be "talked out." For instance, if you've had a number of talks with Jimmy about throwing rocks and the behavior hasn't stopped, it will do no good to talk about it *again*. It's time for other consequences, applied swiftly and fairly.

Disapproval

Sometimes the simplest and most effective tactic of all is to clearly and calmly let your kid know that you disapprove of his behavior. Kids—even that sullen preteen—want and need love and approval. Expressing strong and honest disapproval in a respectful way gets the message across. "Nathan, I'm not happy about you hitting your sister." Hearing his mom's disappointment and anger will make Nathan feel bad about his behavior and resolve to change.

Don't rub it in. Disapproval should not be held like a grudge. Mention it clearly and strongly and leave it at that. But don't be as unassertive as Weak-Willed Winnie, the mom who's afraid to *do* anything lest her kids hate her. When Winnie expresses disapproval, she just can't bring herself to put any "teeth" in it: "Emerald, remember how we talked about how the doll doesn't like it when we set her hair on fire? Emerald, please listen to Mommy. How would you feel if she set your hair on fire? Emerald, darling? The doll might be ruined, dearest. Please, honey pot, it might be a good idea if you put down that can of lighter fluid, darling. Darling? Emmy? *No-o-o-o-o!*"

Warnings

Warnings are not the same as threats (see below under "Mom's Disciplinary No-No's"). You merely need to look at some kids with that certain "look" and say, "I'm warning you," and they'll straighten right up. The old counting trick works for many kids: "I'm counting to 10, now. One…two…three…." By six the kid is scampering. Warnings work when the kid knows the parent will follow through. If you give a warning or start counting, be prepared for the kid to call your bluff. Remember, consistency is vital.

Time-outs or "Thinking Time"

Time-outs, or "thinking time," are a way of "breaking" the action and resetting it on a new track. They remove a child from an environment that's reinforcing the misbehavior. Time-outs are among the must popular techniques for dealing with the misbehavior of small kids. As kids get larger, time-outs become less structured, less, "Take a time-out in the big chair until the timer rings, Alison," and more, "Aaron, you need to take a few moments to cool out. Come back when you can talk to Rachel nicely."

Here are some guidelines for using time-outs:

◆ A time-out is most effective when a child seems to need structure or help changing a mood.

- ◆ A time-out should be imposed immediately and be brief, with the child determining when it's over. Hey, these are good for parents as well as kids!

- ◆ Time-outs should not be used as a punishment or threat, as in, "If you do that again you will get a time-out!"

- ◆ Time-outs should be imposed to remove a child from an environment where she's getting positive feedback for her negative actions. When the child returns, use positive reinforcement for her "improved" behavior to make sure she doesn't step back into the same situation. "Stacey, I like the way you're scratching Spot's belly. Her tail's wagging!"

Separation (From Object)

Sometimes simply "taking it away" is the most effective technique, "it" being whatever object is causing the agony. ("Jonathan and Rebecca, I'm tired of the squabbles. I'm putting the Nintendo up for a while. Please go feed the fish now.") This should not be done in a punitive manner ("I'm taking away the TV, ha ha ha!"), and it should only be done when the object is related to the misbehavior.

Ignoring

It may sound strange, but ignoring is a technique that requires paying attention. When you want to avoid drawing attention to a misbehavior, try actively ignoring it. This technique works best for minor stuff: nose picking, tattling, singing annoying repetitive songs, telling dirty or gross jokes, and the like.

Ignore misbehavior? But...why, Mom? Because it's gentle and it works. Try out this premise for size: Negative attention is better than no attention at all. Think about it. You may have heard this theory in the following context: "Mom, Danny keeps bugging me. He throws spit wads at me across the class." "He's just doing that because he likes you. Just ignore him, and he'll stop doing it."

MOM ALWAYS SAID

Never ignore behavior if the child is harming anything or anybody, including herself.

Be aware that if you choose to "ignore" misbehavior, it will probably get worse before it gets better, as Samantha tries as hard as she can to get a rise out of you. If you use ignoring, you must ignore all instances of the behavior. Once the misbehavior stops, be prepared to actively encourage positive behavior—the behavior that's replacing the misbehavior.

Education

Education uses misbehavior as an opportunity to help move your child from thoughtless to thoughtful. "But why shouldn't I...(smoke, call Jimmy "Chink," play in traffic, and so on)?" Sometimes a child simply doesn't understand the ramifications of a certain misbehavior. All discipline is about learning, but some situations call for a consequence that's specifically educational. A parent who catches her kid smoking might take him to talk with a cancer survivor. One who overhears her child use a racial epithet might get some books on racism, or involve the family in community activities that will introduce them to people from diverse racial groups.

Education is *not* about lecturing. Listen to yourself; do you repeat the same three stories over and over? Kids don't necessarily learn from hearing.

Sometimes you just need to let go and allow your child to gain an education by experiencing the consequences of her actions. Don't compromise on safety, but don't protect your child from reality, either.

"KID GLOVE" TECHNIQUES

There are certain techniques that can be used effectively, but only with great care. I call these the "kid glove" techniques, and they come with warning labels and cautions attached.

Assigning Chores

Chores can be a preventative way to give more responsibility and show a child your trust in him—caring for a family pet, for example. A chore shouldn't be used as a disciplinary consequence unless it's directly related to something a kid did. If the kid trashes the kitchen, yes, it's appropriate to have her clean it up. If she doesn't do her homework, it's not appropriate to have her clean up the kitchen. She should have to do her homework.

Constructive Criticism

The main problem with constructive criticism is that it's very tricky to get the "constructive" part in there. It's very difficult to criticize a child in a way that keeps him feeling good about himself, yet helps him correct his behavior.

Constructive criticism does:

◆ Support, suggest, and educate about the behavior.

◆ Reassure the child that you're upset about the *behavior*, not who he is.

It doesn't:

◆ Scold.

◆ Put down.

◆ Correct with a heavy hand.

Unless you're totally positive that your remarks are helpful, it's best to avoid this not-so-very-positive method.

WISE WORDS

In *constructive criticism*, the critic plays an instructional role. As education *cannot* occur in a hostile climate, constructive criticism *must* be done in a supportive and gentle manner.

Guilt

Ah, guilt. It's like anchovies—a little goes a long way. Guilt has a positive aspect to it. Learning to feel guilty when you're doing something wrong is an important aspect of internalizing discipline and learning self-control. Parents commonly use guilt when they want to tap their child's potential for sympathy toward others. Most people are born with it, but it doesn't necessarily assert itself without help, as most parents find out. So they find themselves saying things like, "You kicked me. See? Now my leg is all bruised and I'll have to miss my aerobics class." Imposing too much guilt on a child can only make her feel resentful, however, and might make her come down too hard on herself.

MOM KNOWS BEST

Don't forget humor! Laughing can relieve tension and stop a kid from "acting out." By joking about it in a nice way, you can call attention to a misbehavior without making it a "heavy" scene.

Withholding Friendliness

This technique is too often used by parents who don't have a warm, close relationship with their kids. It's simple: While your kid misbehaves, you become distant and cold until the behavior improves. I disapprove of this technique because it smacks of holding love hostage to behavior. In theory, your kid, wanting and needing your love and approval, snaps to obedience. In reality, you risk having your child retreat and rebel.

Withholding friendliness only works if:

◆ You have a *very* warm, close relationship.

◆ The withholding is *clearly* specific to the misbehavior.

◆ When the behavior changes, the withholding disappears and you bathe your kid in affection and love. (No sulking or grudges allowed.)

Withholding friendliness is *absolutely not* for use at times when the parent/child relationship is rocky or your kid is otherwise feeling insecure.

MOM KNOWS BEST

If you need to stay involved in a situation but don't want to reward a child's negative behavior with attention, try the poker face—a relaxed body and straight, unimpressed face.

Grounding

"Aw, Mom!" I hear you saying, "Why is grounding in the 'kid glove' group?" Grounding is a very popular consequence, especially for parents of the older child and adolescent. But…it's not always effective, and it must not be overused. Grounding is usually a snap-judgment consequence, imposed in the heat of battle. In other words, grounding is usually a reaction and is often not the best response to a situation.

Here are some of the cons of grounding:

◆ Grounding is rarely related directly to the misbehavior.

◆ Grounding is rarely fully enforced. Most two-week groundings are rapidly forgotten about when the weekend comes.

◆ Grounding is not always enforceable. If you're grounding your 13-year-old daughter, you're effectively grounding yourself.

◆ It isn't necessarily a good teaching tool. Is your child learning why her behavior wasn't appropriate? Is she getting it?

Here are some of the pros of grounding:

◆ It says that actions have consequences.

◆ It can force a busy family to stop, slow down, and spend some time at home. Grounding can turn into family time.

Used correctly as a related response or consequence, grounding can help your child learn to control her own behavior—to call when she's going to be late, to meet her curfew, and so on. When she's shown a lapse in judgment or ability to regulate herself, she needs your guidance to regulate her curfew. That's why it's important that you or another parent stay home *with* her.

Removal of Privileges

Privileges include allowing your child to take on more responsibilities or to do more activities. Grounding is a form of removing privileges; the child loses her freedom for a short period of time. Removal of privileges should not be punitive, and the privileges removed should be clearly in scale with the misbehavior. This method should only be used on a temporary basis, or it will lose its effectiveness.

Before you begin removing privileges as a disciplinary technique or consequence for a misbehavior, you should think about the difference between a child's rights and a child's privileges. Sometimes the line is fuzzy. For example, if Elizabeth has lost a number of library books, it might be appropriate for her to lose the privilege of having a library card. Here's the $20,000 question: Is a library card a right or a privilege?

It's hard to gauge how much responsibility a growing child is ready for. There are bound to be some rough moments. If you've overexpanded the limits and need to pull back, just be careful that your child doesn't feel punished for not being ready to handle more responsibility. This would be a good time to have a problem-solving or brainstorming session. Perhaps you can arrive at a creative solution that will give your kid the structure he needs without making him feel as though he's failed.

MOM'S DISCIPLINARY NO-NO'S

There are all sorts of yucky ways to treat your kids. The list below is not here to make you feel bad; I defy you to show me a parent who hasn't used some—or even many—of these techniques. I list them here for educational purposes. Learn and grow. As you've no doubt realized, Mom, discipline is not just for the kids. It's for the parents, too.

Hurtful Talk

What you say and how you say it can damage your child's sense of self-worth and cause her to question her own sense of self. Here's a list of "don'ts." Mom's first "don't" is for you: Don't use this list to beat yourself up.

- *Yelling.* Yelling? It's not a crime, but just 'cause you do it doesn't mean it's effective! When you're yelling you're certainly not talking *with* your child. All you're communicating is your frustration. Nothing is solved. Your kid may react by feeling angry, intimidated, resentful, or shamed, or he might withdraw and learn to ignore you until you calm down.

- *Sarcasm.* Sarcasm is a cold knife. It puts kids down, builds resentment, and hurts. When a parent is sarcastic, it threatens the child's sense of being loved.

- *Nagging.* Bug, bug, bug. This is not a damaging technique, but it's ineffective. It's kind of like the sense of smell. If you walk into a foul-smelling room, your body will reel with disgust. If you stay in that room for a while, your scent glands will adjust—you'll no longer smell the terrible odor. So it is with nagging. You child will turn you off the way your nose turns off the bad smell. She simply won't hear you anymore.

- *Negative reinforcement: belittling, shaming, generalizing, and name-calling.* "You're turning out just like your Uncle Charles, the convict!" "You're such a baby." "If you eat that extra piece of pie, you'll never find a boyfriend!" "Joe, you're a little slob." "You're a stupid liar." Name-calling *does* hurt. Kids tend to internalize your opinions of them and live up to your expectations. Keep your reinforcements positive.

- *Commanding and demanding.* "Do it right now." "Because I say so." Commands and demands are a show of power, parent over kid. Try for more mutual respect by using requests.

- *Embarrassing/scolding your child in front of friends.* Save it. The idea is to correct the misbehavior in a positive, respectful way. Making your child look bad in front of her friends is humiliating. Of course, once the child is a preteen, anything you do is apt to embarrass her. More on this in Chapter 11.

Setting Traps

Sometimes parents try to trick their kids into lying, or test them to see if, given a seductive situation, they'll misbehave. This is unfair and disrespectful of your child. I'll have more details on effective—and ineffective—ways of handling lying in the next chapter.

Threats and Coercion

Threats are not the same as warnings. "If you don't eat dinner, you'll get no dessert" is a warning—it's valid. It clearly sets the limit and the related consequence. "If you don't get home on time, I'll kill you!" is a coercive threat. It's making a child obey by threatening physical or other harm. Coercion and threats by parents often lead to lying or deception by a child.

Humiliation

Washing a kid's mouth out with soap, making him stand in a corner, sending him to bed without dinner—all these "old" disciplinary techniques humiliate a child and wear down his self-respect.

ALL IN THE FAMILY

 As Nietzche once said (my, my, I *never* thought I'd be quoting Nietzche), "Punishment tames man, but does not make him 'better.'"

Retaliation

Attitude and intention count. What is your intention? Discipline is a positive part of parenting. It should not be done with a vengeful or punishing attitude.

THE CASE AGAINST CORPORAL PUNISHMENT

Spanking, or corporal punishment, is inappropriate and the least desirable way to teach a child discipline. Most parenting experts, including the American Academy of Pediatrics, strongly oppose ever striking a child. I've heard the arguments, old and new, defending spanking. (I'm not talking heavy physical abuse here— see below for that.) Many parents occasionally hit their kids out of fear (the child does something dangerous) or out of stress and frustration. Spanking becomes a problem when it's a common or dominant disciplinary approach. And yes, you can change. Here is the case against corporal punishment:

◆ It doesn't work. It's a short-term solution that often backfires.

◆ It's cruel and painful.

◆ It's harmful emotionally for both parent and child.

◆ It creates resentment.

◆ It does nothing to impart respectful values or standards.

◆ It can lead to body image problems.

◆ It isn't respectful of the child.

◆ It tells a child she's powerless.

◆ It breaks trust, invades a child's sense of security, and halts effective communication.

◆ It teaches children that violence is an acceptable way to express anger or to discipline.

◆ It makes *you* feel like a bully.

WISE WORDS

Corporal punishment means "punishing the body." It's corporal punishment whether you hit your child softly or hard, with your hand or a belt, one time or ten times, frequently or once in a while.

The Defenders Speak and Mom Answers

"Spare the rod, spoil the child."

"Spoiling" is in the eyes of the beholder, but it usually refers to a selfish, demanding child with no sense of sympathy for others. Physical punishment won't teach sympathy; all it teaches is power and betrayal. You "unspoil" a child by setting effective limits and by backing these limits up with fair, just consequences.

"But my kid won't obey unless he knows who's boss!"

I know many parents who are able to keep their kids under "control" and never raise their voices, let alone a hand, to them. If you feel out of control, reevaluate your family rules, limits, and consistency.

"I was so pissed, and she was absolutely hysterical. I gave her just one little whack on the butt and she calmed down."

You've resorted to the power-play to stop a behavior and to vent your own frustrations. One or two occasional swats on the butt aren't going to permanently damage your child. They probably won't be very effective, either. If your kid is wigging out, try gentle physical restraint—bodily holding your child. This may seem counterintuitive when he's screaming that he hates you, but it often works. The flipped-out child is searching for boundaries. Make your arms into loving walls.

"Sometimes the discipline of force is the only thing she'll listen to. It's for her own safety."

Once again, there may be times when you need to use firm, gentle physical restraint. I'll bet that happens *extremely* rarely.

"It was good enough for me!"

Was it really? Replay in your mind what the experience of being spanked was like for you. Did you feel validated, guided, loved, respected, and taught?

Physical Abuse and Attacks

Despite evidence to the contrary, some parents still consider spanking or occasionally swatting a child a valid disciplinary technique. There is no doubt, however, that beating, whipping, hair-pulling, slapping, punching, burning, binding, or other physical attacks on children are never acceptable—and are against the law. Physical abuse—no matter what the parent's intent—causes lowered self-respect, mental health problems, and behavior problems. Evidence suggests that children who have suffered physical abuse often later suffer from delinquency, crime, and violent patterns as abusers and victims.

If you find that you or a parenting partner resort to physical abuse to deal with your child, you need support, and help, to change your parenting habits. Immediately. Please see Chapter 13. Call the Family Violence Prevention Fund at (800) 313-1310.

BE CREATIVE

When it comes to figuring out how to deal with problems and "issues," you've gotta be creative. Think it through, try something, and then try something else. Whatever you do, don't give up hope!

THE LEAST YOU NEED TO KNOW

♦ Flexibility is the key to discipline—different techniques work at different times.

♦ Talking is the first and best response to behavior problems, but effective consequences are often necessary as well.

♦ Disapproval, warnings, time-outs, "taking it away," ignoring, and education are the most effective disciplinary techniques.

♦ All disciplinary techniques should respect the child's dignity, autonomy, and body.

♦ Corporal punishment is ineffective at best, damaging at worst.

9

Mom's Top Disciplinary Complaints (And What to Do About Them)

In This Chapter

- ◆ Dealing with daily difficulties
- ◆ Teaching your kids responsibility without losing your marbles
- ◆ Helping with behavior and relationship problems

Yo! Here's the chapter you've been waiting for—it's all about Mom's top disciplinary complaints and what to do about them. No, *of course* I don't have all the answers. Every child is an individual, every situation is different, and there's no real recipe for discipline. Nonetheless, I'll try to give you a little insight into a variety of situations and potential solutions. As you read through, remember: Always judge the *behavior,* not the *child.*

THE DAILY GRIND

Sometimes it's the little things, the day-in-day-out discipline, that wears your hair thin.

The Bedtime Beast

For many families, bedtime is a major battleground. You're exhausted and you'd love some time alone with your partner. Fat chance, sister. The kids are up and nothing you do is making them go down. Conflict is not the word for this struggle, it's war.

Your child might resist bedtime because:

◆ He wants to continue playing. He rushed out of the house, concentrated at school, did his chores, ate dinner, and did his homework. Now he wants to be a *kid* for a while.

◆ She wants more independence. "Only babies have a bedtime!"

◆ He's a night owl instead of a morning dove. At bedtime, he's just kicking into high gear.

◆ She doesn't need much sleep (hah).

◆ He's using bedtime as an area of rebellion.

So what can you do about it? Well, these guidelines may help:

◆ Let her help determine her own bedtime. If she's 10 years or older and responsible, allowing her some control will make her less prone to rebel. Give her reminders: "Sarah, it's 8:00. You have an hour to finish your homework and get washed up."

◆ Help him with bedtime rituals: bathing, laying out clothes, writing in his journal, and listening to a story.

◆ Set limits and try to avoid nagging. One reminder is enough. "If you're not in bed by 8:30, there will be no time for a story."

◆ Remind her of consequences. Gently point out—don't berate—that the natural result of not sleeping is being tired.

◆ Be there when he's going to bed. Nobody is too old for kisses, cuddles, songs, and stories.

The Morning Moper

Morning hassles can feel worse than the bedtime battles: jangling alarm clocks, grabbing breakfast, bathroom turns, teeth brushing, hair fixing, locating clean socks.... Everybody is stressed, everybody is late, and in the middle of it all sits Molly Moper, completely resistant to the galloping pace. Things disintegrate. Tears and screams this early in the morning can really wreck a day.

Morning hassles are similar to bedtime battles. Some kids just can't get up in the morning. Some don't like to be rushed. Some don't function well when they first wake up. Some are tired from not getting enough sleep. If you've got a morning moper clouding your rising hours, think about these items:

ALL IN THE FAMILY

Five-year-old Heather dug in her heels, refusing to get ready in the morning, while Emma, her responsible nine-year-old sister tried to provide "moral direction." At last Heather put her hands on her hips and faced her sister defiantly. "Emma, you're not my LAWYER!"

◆ How are you in the morning? Remember the power of positive modeling. If mornings are particularly hard for your child, she needs your support. Granted, that's not so easy when you're a grumpy bear, too, or stressed about being late to work *again*.

◆ Look at this as an opportunity: It's your chance to teach Miss Molly some organizational and time-management skills.

◆ Figure out what your kid's trying to tell you. Perhaps your mornings are too rushed and stressful. Your child might be protesting the frantic pace. Nagging and coaxing aren't going to work. They may get him out the door today, but they won't make things any easier tomorrow.

◆ Routines can help. Plan the routine together, perhaps at a family meeting. Try preparing everything the night before—pack the lunch, lay out the clothes, and park the books, backpack, and notes by the door.

- What's going on in her life? Is something unpleasant happening at school or in her social life? She might be stalling to avoid facing the day.

- Give her an alarm clock and suggest that she set it to go off 15 minutes early. Maybe she'll do better if she gets up and plays with her dollhouse for a few minutes before school.

- Consider his "time" temperament and your own. Are you generally late or chronically early? Are you and your child a "fit"?

- Try the Japanese approach: Everybody respects each other's "space," and nobody talks until everybody is fully awake and ready for the day.

- Set consequences. "You're late, you walk."

- Leave each other on a positive note. Cool the screaming and do a little hugging.

- Recognize progress. When your child has done well in the morning, mention it later to reinforce the positive behavior.

MOM KNOWS BEST

 Consider temperament. Some kids are just more challenging than others. Hang in there! And check out Mary Sheedy Kurcinka's book, *Raising Your Spirited Child.*

Food Fights

Eating is a major power-struggle in many families. Our society is obsessed with food and weight. The more you make a fuss about eating, how much you weigh, or how much your child weighs, the more the dinner table will become a battlefield.

In her book *Child of Mine,* Ellyn Satter writes, "You are responsible for what your child is offered to eat, where, and when it is presented. She is responsible for how much of it she eats." Here's the challenge, Mom: To present healthy food and let your children regulate their own intake. It's your job to:

- Model healthy eating and enjoy your food.

- Provide healthy food.

- Don't nag, comment, criticize, praise, or do *anything* except ignore your child's eating patterns. If this is hard for you, take it one meal at a time.

- Share meals. Set a family rule: "This family eats dinner together at least three times a week."

If you think your child might have an eating disorder, get some professional advice. (I've got more information on this in Chapter 11.)

Grooming Gripes

Hair, clothes, and cleanliness are areas where kids feel they can assert some control over their lives. A lot of how your kid wants to look is based on how other kids look. It's part of her *statement.* "Hey, by looking just like everybody else I'm showing what an individual I am!" Try not to get too alarmed. Haul out the pictures of yourself in junior high school. *Then* get alarmed.

Hygiene is a development issue. Eight-, nine-, and ten-year-olds are notorious for being little dirt bags. Once they become adolescents, they tend to spruce up. Then you have the shower battles. "Jim, that's your second 30-minute shower today!"

It's appropriate for you to *set limits* for areas you feel strongly about. ("You *do* need to take a shower before Shabbat.") Problem-solve about areas you're willing to compromise on. (Perhaps you *can* live with a child who washes her hair only once every other week.) And try to make bathing enjoyable. Bubble bath helps; so do fun soaps and interesting water toys.

"Okay, Mom, but what about her *ghastly* taste in clothes?" Look, styles and fads in hair and clothing come and go. Try not to turn them into a battleground. It's important to support as many of your child's choices as possible. Don't be too critical—tell her when she looks good, even when she's wearing something you wouldn't be caught dead in. Here are a few general guidelines:

- Set limits. I remember when the battles were over whether a girl could get her ears pierced! Let him know where certain clothes may be worn and where they are inappropriate.

♦ Put her appearance in context. How else is your kid doing? Purple hair can look damn fine on a kid with a straight-A average and lots of friends.

♦ Consider a clothing allowance. Monthly clothing allowances with spending guidelines can start as young as 10.

♦ Choose your battles. Hair cut and color and some body pierces are revocable—you can undo them. Tattoos are forever.

ALL IN THE FAMILY

 Does your kid really need another pair of $150 athletic shoes? Peer pressure can pressure a family right out of its income. This is a great place to assert your values. Your kid will not suffer irremediable harm if his desires are occasionally denied.

RUTHLESS RESPONSIBILITIES

You want your kid to grow up to be a responsible adult, but oh, your aching head! How will you get through all the years of whining and complaints?

Chores—What a Bore!

There's a wide range of opinion about chores. Most parents believe that kids should help out around the house. Some pay their kids, some don't. Some parents feel it's not worth the agony of trying to get their kids to do the chores and then having to do them over themselves because they were done so poorly. Some families assign chores; some ask their kids to help as the need arises.

Chores are often fraught with procrastination and grumbling. Sometimes this chore resistance is simply because the child is "overworked"—too much homework, activities, and scheduled time. However, don't rule out a natural human aversion to work of any kind. And don't get mad about it either. Do *you* like to do housework?

When chores aren't done well, reconsider your expectations. Perhaps she doesn't know *how* to squeegee the shower. Teach her, be patient, and give positive reinforcement for what she *does* do. One of the problems with chores is that they tend to be boring. Make them a family affair—clean the house together! If all else fails, relax, you're not a bad mom. Most kids don't do chores until college—and many don't do them even then!

Homework Hassles

Some kids do homework easily; for others it's hard. They may need your help. If you're actively involved in their school life (school visits, checking in with them as they do their homework), you'll have an easier time telling when the problem is with the concept of "doing homework" and when your child is really stuck in the material. Here are other things to bear in mind:

- ◆ It's hard for active kids who have been sitting in school all day to come home and sit all afternoon or evening doing homework. Consider a planned exercise break.

- ◆ Children under 10 need involvement but not too much help. Remain a little distant; don't take over their projects. Don't try to be their teacher—they've already got at least one at school!

- ◆ Children get lonely locked in the wee garret slaving for hours over social studies. Make homework part of family life: Let them do homework in the family room or the kitchen. You can walk by, ruffle some hair, and be available for questions.

- ◆ Don't reward procrastination.

BEHAVIORS AND RELATIONSHIPS

The biggest disciplinary complaints fall into the category of behaviors and relationships. Here are some ideas.

Problem: Bullying

The bully is a child who feels out of control in his life and who feels he must bully others to get what he needs and wants. Bullying usually has a boomerang effect; the bully's friends usually dump him, leaving the bully feeling even worse about himself.

Solution:

◆ Don't label your child a bully. Don't let others label him a bully.

◆ Give support, not censure. This doesn't mean pity. If his friends stop being his friends, gently let him know why. Try a problem-solving session, and talk with him about ways to get his friends back or make new ones.

◆ Offer help with social skills. The bully doesn't fully know how to contribute and share with others.

◆ Consider professional help. Chronic aggression may be a sign of a learning disability or other problems (see Chapter 13).

MOM KNOWS BEST

Bullying is common among siblings. Empower the bullied sibling by acknowledging what's going on. "John wasn't letting you do your own art project, was he. I'll speak with him about that."

Problem: Cheating

Cheating tends to brings out rage in parents. If your kid is caught cheating, you may remain suspicious for months. Actually, cheating is very common. After all, surveys show that up to 70 percent of all students admit to having cheated at least once in high school. Kids get the message very early that this is a dog-eat-dog world and that they're expected to achieve. Cheating can mean that a child is having trouble with parental expectations. Or a child may see it as a quick way out of a problem.

Solution:

◆ Don't label her a cheater.

◆ Let him know that cheating is not acceptable. (This is the time to look at your own behavior. What are you modeling? Do you cheat on taxes, keep the extra change, or cut ahead in line? Is there tacit approval for cheating behavior?)

◆ Check the pressure. Cheating is often a sign that too much emphasis is being placed on grades or winning. Try non-competition for a while.

◆ Show sympathy for the stress your child may be under.

◆ Don't confront. You risk giving her the opportunity to lie (see "Problem: Lying," later in this chapter).

◆ Look for the positive intent and then offer help. If your child is cheating on homework, she may feel panicked and behind. Does she need a tutor? Does she need help with her study habits?

Problem: Cruelty

Bullying is more common among boys, while girls tend to express aggression through cruelty and psychological warfare. Cruelty often takes the forms of excluding other kids and saying mean things. Where's the positive intent here? Well, being part of the group is very important for kids, and one way to assure inclusion is to exclude others. (Not a very good way, I might add.) In fact, children often exclude others because they've been excluded themselves.

Cliques are part of the developmental process, alas. All kids feel unpopular at times, some more than others. When your child feels excluded, you can help by listening, listening, listening. Advice is probably *not* very helpful. Get her involved in other activities: scouts, art classes, or weekend team sports. She may do better with a different group of kids.

Solution:

If you see your child being cruel, show clear disapproval of what's going on. You can help your child—if she's being cruel or is the target of cruelty—by encouraging her and supporting her efforts to reach out to friends: invite them for dinner, for overnights, and to special events.

Problem: Disobedience

All kids are disobedient sometimes. It's a way for them to learn about and express themselves, to discover their own boundaries, and to test your boundaries (arghhh!!). If your child is occasionally disobedient, she may be seeking clearer limits or consequences. If the pattern of disobedience is new or chronic, it's time to figure out what's going on.

Solution:

Is there a lot of fighting, hitting, and yelling in your household? How's the "respect" level? Talk to her. What's happening at school? Tell her you sense she's having a hard time in her life, then listen, listen, listen. You're both in this together. Let her know you're an ally, not an enemy.

If your child is chronically disobedient, consider getting some help. Check out Chapter 13 for more ideas.

Problem: Swearing

Virtually all kids go through stages of swearing to the point where it's considered almost a developmental norm. Kids swear to be cool, impress their friends, and shock adults.

Solution:

Be careful what you're modeling. How's *your* language? Once you've checked your own reality, here's an area where ignoring (see Chapter 8) can be useful. Treat swearing as though it's not a big deal and it probably won't be. Keep in mind, though, that there's a difference between using swear words and swearing *at* somebody. Name-calling is *not* respectful.

Problem: Lying

Yes, honesty is an important value, one we want to instill in our children. When your little one stares you in the face and tells a bald-faced lie, it can feel like a betrayal. If she keeps it up, you may feel shocked, angry, or even that you've failed as a parent.

Try not to worry too much about lying, and try not to focus too much on the behavior. Kids—and adults—lie for a wide variety of reasons:

♦ From fear of consequences or punishment. This sometimes happens when rules are too stringent or expectations are too high. (Review the material in Chapter 2.)

♦ To protect themselves or somebody else.

♦ Reflex. Sometimes a person doesn't mean to tell a lie; she's surprised in a misdeed and it just "slips out."

♦ To impress and win love and approval.

Solution:

The best approach to preventing lies is to avoid creating a situation where your kid feels pressured to choose between lying or suffering. Lies are a misguided survival technique. After all, a cornered animal will fight fiercely; a trapped animal will chew through his own leg to get free. Keep in mind the following:

♦ Ixnay on the cross-examinations. "Andre, where were you on the night of January 14?" won't get Andre to open up and talk.

♦ Keep the focus of the conversation on the problem or event, not on casting blame.

♦ Encourage and praise the child for telling the truth. Confessions take a lot of courage. Apply reasonable consequences for the misdeed—if you've praised her for her honesty, the consequence will be easier to take—but make her feel good about doing the right thing.

♦ Don't force a confrontation. If you're certain that John has done something wrong, standing in front of him with a threatening look on your face and saying, "JOHN, DID YOU BREAK THE TV?" virtually compels him to lie. He can't win. Whatever he says will be a disaster. If he says yes, he'll suffer your anger. If he says no, you'll accuse him of lying. A better approach would be, "John, let's talk about the TV. What happened?"

MOM KNOWS BEST

If you're going to talk to your child about lying, make sure you *know* you're right. Kids have a strong sense of injustice and unfairness, and false accusations can rankle for years.

"But my kid does lie!" I hear you protest. When lying happens, try not to focus on the lie, or on the distressing fact that your child isn't being honest. This can be hard. I've heard many irate parents say things like, "I can understand how you could have torn my poster down, but I can't tolerate the fact that you lied to me about it." If you know your child is lying to you:

◆ Let the child know that you know the truth, in as casual a tone as you can muster.

◆ Don't label her a liar. Even if you know your kid has lied, don't call names. Kids internalize labels, and a negative one like "liar" can hurt and damage her.

◆ Breathe. Take some time to calm down. Take a break, a walk, anything that will enable you to come back and deal with the situation rather than the lie.

◆ Remember that lies are easily compounded. Give your kid the benefit of the doubt—she may have slipped into a little lie and found herself in way over her head. Wait until the situation she lied about is resolved. Then initiate a conversation (not a lecture) about the problems lying can cause.

What about consistent, compulsive lying? Try reassessing your discipline expectations. Are you being reasonable in your requests? Or is your child perhaps getting undue attention for her lying?

Look at what else is happening in your child's life. Perhaps there's a reason she wants to escape into fantasyland. Chronic lying is a symptom of other problems; it's rarely an isolated problem itself.

Problem: Running Away from Home

Running away has been glorified in books, movies, and miniseries as the beginning of a grand adventure. In reality, running away is terribly dangerous and scary for all involved.

Solution:

Always take "running away" threats seriously. Don't call your child's bluff or be sarcastic. (Some parents actually pack their kids' bags and then stand in the doorway saying, "Good-bye!" This is not a good idea.) If your child does run away, look for her *immediately.* It's too risky to let her find her own way back.

Once your child returns (or is returned) home, you'll need to address his pain. It's vital to deal with whatever made him leave in the first place. Running away is a drastic step. What's going on in your child's life that he would rather run away than face? If necessary, seek professional support.

Problem: Sibling Slaughter

Can you leave your kids alone together? Fighting among siblings is one of the most common problems families face. Yet minor rivalry can be a healthy and important socialization experience for your kids—it's a way for them to practice conflict resolution in a safe environment.

Solution:

- Treat your children equally. (That doesn't mean "the same.")
- Put limits on rivalry and bickering. "In this family we stick up for each other."
- Don't make one sibling responsible for the other if you can help it.
- Make sure siblings have activities alone and together.

ALL IN THE FAMILY

Parental attitudes help shape the sibling relationship. Some parents even express preferences: "Abel is a great kid, but Cain is just like his Uncle Bert, a no-good." How is Cain going to feel about his brother, Abel? Talk about sibling rivalry!

Problem: Stealing

Stealing, like lying and cheating, is very common among kids. It doesn't matter how well you understand this, though. If your kid is caught stealing, you're probably going to be angry, shocked, and embarrassed. Most stealing is occasional. If your child steals frequently, or the stealing is combined with other misbehaviors, you may need to seek professional help. Kids steal for a variety of reasons:

♦ To impress friends. Stealing can also be a response to friends—a.k.a., peer pressure.

♦ Desire. Maybe he just wanted something he or you couldn't afford.

♦ Shame. He might have been afraid to ask you for the money, or felt too embarrassed to buy the desired object (condoms, Playboy magazine...).

♦ Stress. Is anything else going on in your child's life?

Solution:

If your child is caught stealing, it's time to have a talk about why he's stealing. Be open about your disapproval and your values, but don't ridicule or embarrass him. He'll just tune out. Have him make restitution, returning the merchandise and paying for damages.

Remember, your first job is to be your child's ally. If she has committed a small theft, you need to teach her that this is wrong, but you also need to protect her. Some stores have a "no-tolerance" policy. In this case, you'll have to decide whether you think a night in jail and a record is in your child's best interest. Perhaps it is. If not, you might be able to "make a deal" for restitution that teaches the desired lesson but doesn't have lifelong consequences.

Put a child who has been caught stealing "on notice." Let her know you're watching her behavior and that she has lost some trust and needs to earn it back.

Problem: Talking Back

The child who is sassy, stands up for herself, and "talks back" gets mixed responses from adults, especially in the United States. She can infuriate, but her spirit will also capture respect: This child won't get run over as a grown-up!

Almost all children will sometimes "talk back" to provoke a reaction in you, but increased incidents of "talking back" could mean she's having difficulty dealing with stress or is very angry about something in her life. And sometimes sass is just sass. All kids are impudent on occasion.

Solution:

The family rules apply here. It's okay for a child to express her feelings; it's not okay for her to do so in an abusive manner.

Problem: Tattling

Tattling is most common between siblings. No parent wants a tattletale child; for one thing, tattlers tend to be unpopular with other kids. Kids generally tattle for revenge, to gain attention or favor, or to wield power.

Solution:

- Label the behavior as tattling and let her know you don't approve.

- Ignore tattling. When siblings tattle on each other, try not to get drawn in. Say, "We don't tattle on each other. Work it out yourselves." Keep a poker face while you say it. Leave the room.

- Help chronic tattlers with their interpersonal skills.

- Don't scold a child whose behavior you haven't seen; it gives too much power to the tattler.

MOM KNOWS BEST

Tattling is not the same as speaking out against injustice. Let your child know that it's *always* okay to tell if somebody is being hurt or is unsafe. Reassure him that he can always come to you if he's scared.

THE LEAST YOU NEED TO KNOW

♦ Always judge the behavior, not the child.

♦ The small bits of day-in-day-out discipline can sometimes feel the most challenging. Remember to breathe.

♦ Let the little things slide. Save your battles for the big ones!

♦ Lying, stealing, and bullying behavior are not uncommon. Your kid is *not* the only one!

♦ Behavior and relationship problems are opportunities for teaching—when you approach them calmly.

10

The Disciplining Duo

In This Chapter

◆ How to discipline with a partner

◆ Stepmomhood—when you're the mom, when you're the step

◆ Disciplining with caregivers, other parents, and teachers

To dream...the American Dream...hah. The pressure to form the "standard" household—one mom, one dad, one boy, one girl, one dog or cat, and one white picket fence—has gone the way of rotary phones, and good riddance. The new American family is so much more interesting! And it comes in such a wide variety of shapes, sizes, and permutations. Step right up, get yer blended family! How about yer single-parent household? Or yer household with two moms or two dads? Sample a family that includes grandparents or other adults. Make up your own combination—mix 'n' match!

Yes, families today come in a variety of forms. Yet, no matter *what* the size or configuration of your family, you've probably got at least one *parenting partner.* Some moms have many. Your spouse or lover, your baby-sitter, your child's teacher, your child's coach, your own parents, your involved siblings, your ex's new spor, the parents of your children's friends—all these parenting pa have involvement, and influence, in your kid's life. In thi<

117

I offer a few clues and details about teaching discipline with a parenting partner.

WISE WORDS

A *parenting partner* is anybody who shares parenting or child care with you, including any adults who have direct involvement with or influence on your child's life.

THE PARENTING DUO

Here they come, that dynamic duo, the two parents! When there are two of you doing the parenting, the most important issues are commitment and consistency. If your family is like a body, think of you and your co-parent as the body's two hands. (That's an appropriate metaphor, right? The hands do most of the work...) Remember the saying, "The right hand doesn't know what the left hand is doing?" That's what you want to avoid.

In the discussion that follows, I'll be talking about *her* and *him*, but of course this advice goes for any parenting combination.

Developing a Unified Front

Consistency is vital. If you're not consistent, your kids are going to play you off, one parent against another. Gruesome. Given your busy life, you're not going to be able to check in with your parenting partner for every little issue or incident. Aha! You've got to plan ahead! This requires talking about joint discipline ("No! No! Anything but that, Mom!") and developing a unified front. Working out the united front will probably require more than one "big talk." Hey, parenting—and discipline—is a process. For example: Bob and Ellen tell Patty she's too young to date, though Ellen feels ambivalent. Meanwhile, she and Bob continue to negotiate. That's a unified front.

Here are some suggestions for making the "big talks" less of an deal:

mbine them with pleasure: Go to a cafe to chat or sit around fireplace in the evening. When you're relaxed and in a nood, you'll be able to discuss joint discipline sanely.

◆ *Know that discipline is a difficult area for* all *parents.* If tempers heat up, it's because you both are passionate people. (If things get too hot, try taking a break, concentrating on the passion, and leaving the discipline for another day.)

◆ *Try to anticipate potential problem areas.* The idea is to be explicit with each other about your family's rules and behavioral expectations. Make a plan. Try and establish a general set of guidelines.

◆ *Ideally, your shared values extend to a positive approach to discipline.* What if you love your partner and think he's *very* sexy (even with that thinning hair and little pudgy paunch), but boy, does he blow it on the discipline front? Well, discipline is about learning—for the entire family. The two of you may have to have a little problem-solving session on your own. (Remember problem-solving in Chapter 5?)

◆ *As much as possible, avoid having one person make unilateral decisions,* especially if you tend to disagree.

◆ *Agree on good faith.* Make a deal that if your partner makes and acts on a parenting decision, you're going to stand behind it, even if you disagree, and he'll do the same for you. (Take it up with your partner later.)

When Issues Arise

Of course you can't anticipate everything. When 11-year-old Jason asks to go to a mixed-gender slumber party or 8-year-old Sarah paints the walls of her room purple without asking, it's time for the parents to talk. Are you going to do it in private or where Jason or Sarah can hear and see the decision-making process? Will they be a part of this process, or will the parents be a unified front, announcing what they've decided?

Where and when do you and your parenting partner figure out the correct course of action? Some parenting partners include the child, and some do not. Here's a sample of each approach. It's up to *you* to decide what's most appropriate for a specific situation.

1. Private Parenting with Esther and Frank

Esther and Frank discuss *every* problem before saying yes or no. If their two boys ask them something, they say, "We'll discuss it," and disappear into the bedroom. All Frank Jr. and Easton hear is the occasional hiss. A while later, Esther and Frank emerge, a unified front, and make their pronouncement.

Pros: No chance that Frankie Jr. and Easton can pit one parent against the other *here*. These parents are obviously very tuned into each other and committed to consistency.

Cons: The kids are growing up with little idea how the process of solving conflict works. They may not even know if there *is* conflict. They're out of the loop.

2. Battling It Out with Bob and Terry

Bob and Terry believe they should be as open as possible with their kids and that all family members are equal members. If a disciplinary situation arises, the family talks about it together. When Bob and Terry disagree about the right way to handle an issue, they argue it out—loudly. When they come to a solution, everybody knows how they achieved it.

Pros: The kids, Tommy, Hank, and Mariah, are learning that people who love each other can successfully argue, yell, disagree, and then problem-solve their way to a solution.

Cons: There are some privacy issues here—the kids are on trial in front of everybody. Because the parents aren't providing a unified front, people are open for side-taking. Life in this family can feel like a battle zone. Mean things may be said.

3. The Happy Medium

Ideally, parenting partners discuss some issues in private and some with their children present or participating—perhaps at family meetings. Of course, the individual situation will help determine your approach.

React...or Wait?

If you're in a parenting partnership and an important disciplinary issue comes up when you're alone with your child, you may want to wait to make a decision until you and your partner have had a chance to hash it out. It's a rush, rush, rush world, and people tend to feel like they have to make a decision now! Most of the time, important things can wait. Be the first on your block to slow down.

When the situation calls for a quick, unilateral decision, however, you'll *know why* you spent that time discussing guidelines with the other parent. And, since you've discussed your general philosophy with your partner, said partner will understand why you decided Martina could eat an entire cheesecake before dinner.

Trusting the Bozo You Married

Trusting your co-parent to do the right thing is hard. What about when it's the other parent who makes the split-second decision? Hey, life is about letting go and trusting. You do what you can to make sure everybody is reading from the same menu, then you let it go. People have different ways of doing things, even within a family. For instance, even though Sarah and Lee agree that Maurice should help around the house, they have different ideas about what that means. When Sarah is supervising, 10-year-old Maurice scrubs toilets and cooks dinner. When Lee is in charge, Maurice dries the lettuce and gets praised for getting his dirty socks in instead of near the laundry basket.

"But he's wrong, wrong, wrong!" you wail. Hey, so work on it. Discipline is hard. It requires a commitment to working out the issues, and, yes, sometimes things go badly. Let's be candid: Differences in child rearing and discipline are a big cause of divorce. It's worth it to spend the time (and, if you go to a therapist, the money) to save and enhance your marriage.

MOM KNOWS BEST

Priorities differ. If one parent feels super-strong about an issue and the other doesn't really care, the one who feels stronger about the situation should take priority.

"But Dad Said..."

It's great to talk about consistency and providing a united front; it's a lot harder to keep kids from trying to drive a wedge between you. Here's the simple scenario: You say no. Alphonse goes to Daddy. Alphonse doesn't say, "I asked Mommy and she said no," Alphonse just asks again. And Daddy, in his innocence, says.... Well, whatever Daddy says, the fact that you've raised such a devious offspring is gonna bug you. Keep in mind:

◆ A certain amount of manipulation is normal and healthy. Manipulation is a common way for kids to gain control over their lives. Remember that kids are essentially powerless over the large adults who have so much power over them.

◆ You don't have to play into it. Train yourself and your co-partner to say, "Let me check with (Dad, Mom, Susan, or whoever is involved with you in this joyous activity called parenting)."

"Wait Until Dad Gets Home!"

You know the old scenario: The kids misbehave and Mom blows up, yells and screams, and then cuts loose with the fateful words, "Just wait until your Dad comes home!" This is not a great way to handle problems. It puts *all* the disciplining responsibility on Dad, it represents you as an unassertive parent, and it sets up your kid to expect punishment.

You don't need to decide what to do about a situation immediately. It's fine—appropriate even—to talk with your partner about it, but don't leave your kid hanging in a state of nervous dread. That's cruel. At *least* have a little talk about it when it happens.

Who's the Bad Cop Tonight?

When your kid has a behavior problem or has done a big nasty no-no, the first thing you do is talk about it, right? Sometimes, though, two people talking about a problem at once seems like too much. You don't want to gang up on the poor child. On the other hand, you also don't want to take on permanent roles, with one parent playing the angel while the other gets to be the big bad b...witch. If you can, take turns. If you've shown your unified front, your kids won't feel that one parent is evil and one is not. You'll be known as a disciplining unit.

ALL IN THE FAMILY

 Life for single moms can be tough. It does offer one advantage, though: You do get to discipline your way and do it consistently. This means you can have real influence. You can also choose your male role models— uncles, friends, grandfathers....

DISCIPLINE AFTER DIVORCE

If discipline were a college major, then "Discipline After Divorce" would be an upper-division course. No doubt about it, it can be *hard*. Parents often have differences of opinion when it comes to disciplinary issues. When there's been a split-up, those differences may be magnified. There's often resistance to cooperation. (Some of it may even be coming from you!) A lot of your success as divorced co-parents will depend upon how committed both parents are to keeping the child out of the middle and how committed you both are to the best interests of your kids. Though you know you *should* cooperate for the best interests of the kids, for many this is much easier said than done. If you're sharing disciplinary duty with an ex, the reminders below might help:

◆ *What's happening at the ex's house?* Disciplinary details may often be unclear or missing. For example, Emily comes home to you complaining that her dad isn't allowing her to have a party because she overlooked a dirty sock when she was cleaning her room. Resist the impulse to curse the jerk of a man you mistakenly married years ago. Emily may not be giving you all the background. She may also not *know* her dad's rationales.

◆ *Don't try to remedy the other parent's disciplinary misdeeds unless you perceive a danger to your child.* Support your child and do the best you can at *your* house. We all have our burdens in life. Yours may be to help pay for your child's years on the psychiatrist's couch.

♦ *When you disagree with a disciplinary action that your ex takes, try to deal with him privately and respectfully.* Don't badmouth your ex's discipline in front of your child. You'll put her in the difficult position of being forced to choose sides.

Finally, remember that while the divorce is still "fresh," you may see more behavioral problems. Divorce is like an injury: Wounds need to heal, and it's not easy to predict what form this will take. Talk to your child's school (coach, dance teacher…) about what's going on and agree to keep each other informed about changes in behavior.

STEPMOMHOOD

You're a stepmom? Yow, that's a kicker. I give you my congratulations and lend you all my strength. It's a hard row to hoe, particularly when it comes to discipline. What's your right? What's your role? What power do you have in this situation? Luckily, you're not alone. Blended families are more and more common. That means more and more women are doing what you're doing—trying to parent without being typecast as The Evil Stepmother. They say it takes up to seven years to blend a family completely. So how are you going to handle discipline, the trickiest of all parenting tasks? Here are some suggestions for getting through the rough spots:

♦ *Defer to the biological parents.* Yes, you have a say—you have influence—but the kids, you, and your relationship will do better if you butt out for a few years. This is very hard to do for many moms. Diana, a strong, outspoken stepmom, had to bite her tongue—sometimes literally—for the first two years of stepmomhood. She knew that Keisha and Bronson, her stepchildren, would listen to their dad but would resent her if she tried to correct their behavior. She used ignoring and gave a lot of encouragement and praise. Eventually she gained their trust and was able to assert herself in a way they didn't resent.

◆ *Be the power behind the throne.* There's nothing wrong with dragging your partner into the bedroom to hiss disciplinary suggestions. Discuss it. Your partner should be your ally and vice versa. Just because he's the biological dad doesn't mean you shouldn't have *some* say. You live there, after all.

◆ *Don't badmouth the mom.* It won't gain you any friends, and it may generate resentment. And then they'll *never* listen to you!

◆ *All of this having been said, don't be a pushover.* It's important that your stepkids see you as an authority figure and that they see you and their biological parent as a disciplinary unit. You *may* have to step in and assert yourself. (You may also have to resolve some issues with your partner first.)

◆ *Establish a different role for yourself.* Sarah grew up with her mother's three sisters as powerful and present figures in her life. Her aunts, through their gentle guidance and suggestions, had almost as much influence on her behavior as her mother. When she became the stepmom of two kids, she remembered her aunts and modeled her behavior—and disciplinary style— after theirs.

When the Kid Lives with You

When your stepchild lives with you, you have some real authority. After all, it's your house, too. The danger comes when you assert yourself too much, especially early in the stepfamily relationship. You *can* get heard—that's what family meetings and family rules are for, right?

Family meetings, family rules, special time, and family time are great ways to speed the "blending" process and make sure that you and the other members of the family are having your needs met. (See Chapters 4 and 5 to review these topics.)

Your stepkid will feel a bit like a fish out of water in "your" house, especially if the split-up is fairly recent. Encourage her to participate in family decisions, asking for her input when decorating a room, for example. Make sure she has a private place she can call her own. Respecting a child's privacy shows respect for the child, and respect is a *big* part of teaching discipline.

Stepmoms and Shared Custody

Shared custody can be a challenge. Transition times when the kid is switching houses (and parental units) are usually the hardest—expect more behavioral problems, and be lenient. Think of it as a storm blowing through your house, and wait for the wind to blow away the clouds. Above all, try to show—and feel—sympathy for the child, who has to negotiate two ways of doing everything.

If your stepchildren don't live with you full- or part-time, you'll probably have to deal with "The Visit." (Cue the scary music.) You may see some very ugly things, especially at the dinner table. Don't tolerate gross behavior, but try to be lenient. Even if you don't approve of the behavior patterns, it won't help to try to change things for a short, occasional visit, and it will cause resentment. When you can't stand it anymore, you can assert yourself by making a general assertion of the rules: "At our house, we don't have food fights."

When You're the Mom

A stepmom can feel like a total intrusion into your territory. Who is this bimbo anyway, and what is she teaching *your* kids? Buck up, and keep the following in mind:

- *Take a leap of faith.* You have tremendous influence on your children. The "other woman" might challenge that influence, but she won't threaten it. Every person your child meets in life has something to offer—good or bad—that you can't. All you can do is teach them the best you can, then let them go.

- *Don't badmouth the stepmom.* Take the high road; it will reflect better on you, and you won't put your kid in the awkward position of feeling like he needs to *hate* her. He has to spend time with her; you don't. Like it or not, she's in your kid's life.

- *Try to deal with your ex directly rather than the new stepmom* if you have a difference in disciplinary approach or are having some issues about what's going on in the other household.

- *She's not necessarily your enemy.* Because she comes from a different perspective, she may actually be a good ally. Enlist her. Call and be friendly (she'll probably be so shocked she'll pass out). You can try for a face-to-face discussion, but don't be surprised if you're met with a chilly reception.

MOM KNOWS BEST

It's best for the kids if the parents—biologicals and steps—get along. Grit your teeth, take the high road, and don't gossip or badmouth in front of the kids.

DISCIPLINE AND OTHER PEOPLE

Hillary Rodham Clinton says, "It takes a village to raise a child," and Mom agrees. However, in any village there are not only the neighbors, the teacher, the coach, the doctor, the police officer, the postal inspector, the butcher, the baker, and the candlestick maker, there are also the town gossip, the weird old man who lives behind the mill, and the meddlers. In other words, not *everybody* should have a say in your child's upbringing. Especially in the area of discipline.

The Meddlers

You'll know it when you meet a meddler because meddlers are never silent. The meddler's whispers follow you throughout the store. "If she was my daughter, I'd whip her good for talking to the checker like that." Or, "That mom has lost control of her child. Look at what that child is wearing—black lipstick! Whatever is next?" Part of you scoffs. You're dealing with the situation (whatever it may be). You're the parent; you know what's going on, they don't. Who cares what they think? Another part of you cringes. You're human, you want approval, and you especially want approval for your parenting.

It can be hard to deal with other opinions. Make your decisions and hold firm. You're doing it for your *kids*.

Teachers and Coaches

Trouble? A teacher or a coach, somebody who cares about your kid, who has some influence and clout in her life but who doesn't go home with her every night, can be just the ticket. She may not listen to you (you're her *mom,* for crying out loud), but she'll listen to her coach.

John and Angela's 12-year-old son, Corbin, was in love with another student. Corbin and his girlfriend were deep in over their heads, reading *Romeo and Juliet* and talking about running away to elope. Their grades dived, they lied about seeing each other, and they sneaked out at night to be together. The families flipped out! Finally, they called in Corbin's school counselor to sit down with the families and the kids and work out a solution.

The kids were good students who cared about their futures. At the strong urging of the counselor, who had some clout over the destinies of both, they agreed to a series of compromises about how much contact they could have with each other. Corbin and his girlfriend were actually relieved to have limits set, and both sets of parents felt much better about the situation.

This approach worked because Corbin and his girlfriend respected and agreed with the counselor's ideas and perspectives. It's not that they rejected their parents. Sometimes kids find it easier to listen to *anybody* and his stepbrother twice removed than their own mom and dad.

People who are concerned and involved in your child's life but have some distance from the situation may be able to see more clearly what's going on. Then again, sometimes people are wrong. Let your own good sense be your guide.

Other Parents

Let's all say it together this time: "Flexibility is good." And exposure to other people's parenting styles is great flexibility training for your child. (Hey, you may look terrific in comparison!) Most parents will be respectful of your child's personal space. Even the ones who might use corporal punishment on their own children will probably not use it on yours. These parents use corporal punishment because on some level they believe their children to be their "property," and they will respect your "property." Besides, it's against the law.

Unfortunately, it's not against the law to berate another parent's child. The best advice for this situation is to keep the lines of communication open so that your child feels he can come to you if something weird or uncomfortable happens with another adult.

Extended Family

Though it's far less common than it used to be, extended family members—Grandma, Aunt Jane, Uncle Rio—have long been involved in the rearing of children. But how do you deal with it when Grandma slaps Suzy's palm with a ruler for grabbing too many cookies?

◆ *You* are the mom. You decide how you want your child to be raised and "disciplined." Decide on your "bottom line," the line over which you will not go, and inform the other adults. Some things are not negotiable. "*Nobody* hits my child."

◆ Understand that different people have different approaches to child-rearing and that, along with the wonderful advantages of having extended family in your child's life, there are some decided disadvantages. Things don't always get done your way.

◆ You may be teaching discipline differently from the way you were disciplined as a child. If your parents are active participants in your child's life, there may be struggle. Consider it an opportunity for education and for testing your own flexibility. Different people have different styles. So long as those styles don't offend your moral sense or cause danger to your child, your children will benefit from the variety of experiences. You can always talk things over with the child later. "Grandma believes children should be seen and not heard. We believe that everybody gets a turn to talk, but when we're at Grandma's house, try not to interrupt."

◆ Remember that you are your child's *ally*, and being an ally may mean standing up for him, even if it becomes uncomfortable for you. "Dad, Joey has a right to his opinion!"

WISE WORDS

An *ally* is somebody you can count on—whenever and however. An ally might be a friend, a relative, or a stranger. Allies can be more important than friends.

THE LEAST YOU NEED TO KNOW

◆ No matter what the size or configuration of your family, you probably have at least one parenting partner to work with.

◆ Work with your parenting partner to develop a unified front.

◆ You don't have to make most parenting decisions on-the-spot. Take your time, and consult with your parenting partner.

◆ If you're a stepmom, or if you have one in your life, things can get complicated. Keep the kids' interests front and center, and be patient. It takes time.

◆ Teachers, coaches, and other adult friends can be your child's allies at times when you cannot.

Adolescence Strikes!

Adolescence. First there are the physical changes: bodies stretching, swelling, sprouting hair, and springing smells. Look at your kid one month, he's a little kid. The next, it's like looking in a fun house mirror! Who is this gangly, pimply, distorted version of your beautiful baby? Well, if he *looks* weird, imagine what's going on inside. He's got a whole new body to get used to and a whole new set of hormones. The internal, emotional changes you can't see are even more dramatic, probably, than the physical ones you can see. And just as he (and you) starts to get acclimated, everything changes again.

OH, NO! SHE'S TURNING INTO A, A...

It's kind of like "morphing," the computer technology they use in Hollywood for certain kinds of special effects. Morphing is what transforms a Star Trek security officer into gelatin, a woman into a can of chicken noodle soup, and Michael Jackson into a panther. If you freeze the video in the middle of a morph, the image looks completely bizarre—a little like the original image, a little like the final image, and *more* than a little confusing and monstrous.

That's what is happening to your child. Adolescence is a slow-motion morph from child to adult.

Let me put a more clichéd spin on it: She's a butterfly emerging from a chrysalis, an ugly duckling becoming a swan. Becoming, emerging, changing. Adolescence is a bridge whose far end is shrouded in mist. What's over there? Who will this child become? It's more than a little exciting watching her begin the journey across that bridge and seeing the far end of it begin to clear as she gets closer to it.

Discipline is about teaching your child to internalize the discipline. Part of being an effective teacher is letting your student go forth boldly, bearing his knowledge. Your young adolescent isn't wearing the cap and gown of self-discipline yet—far from it—but he's beginning to stretch out on his own. You can begin widening his limits. That's right, Mom. It's time to start practicing the graduation march.

Is This Really Necessary?

Adolescence is when children really begin to come into their own, to figure out who they are. Whether you look at the changes your child is going through as a beautiful emergence or a horrific nightmare, you'll need new tactics to deal with problems—a new approach to dealing with your child. In this chapter, I hope to give you a peek into the inside world of the adolescent—its beautiful vistas and its deep, terrifying gorges.

Even the healthiest and most well-adjusted adolescent needs to push hard to establish her autonomy. It's her job to separate; it's your job to remain sane while she does it. The best way to avoid flipping out and making yourself miserable is to get educated about "normal" rebellion. Then you'll be able to help prevent—or deal with—the more destructive and self-destructive forms.

When Does It Start?

Adolescence (like morphing) is a process. It begins for different kids at different times, and it's not just the physical effects of puberty; it's a social thing as well. I've known 12-year-olds who are deeply involved in the dating scene and 15-year-olds who are barely starting to emerge from their world of imaginary play.

Many parents dread adolescence. They're sure that when the full moon comes out, their kid will grow hair and fangs and run around biting people. Michael Riera, author of *Uncommon Sense for Parents with Teenagers,* says, "Adolescence is not a phase of life to be feared; rather, it is one of fascination, curiosity, and unexpected twists." Riera believes that parents and teenagers possess "different world views that inform their behaviors, attitudes and interpretations of events in very different ways." He also stresses that teenagers don't want an adversarial relationship any more than parents do. Part of your job as Reasonable Mom is to remember that your adolescent child, like the werewolf, is not exactly, and not always, of the same species you are. Sometimes your adolescent will require inter-species communication strategies.

Letting Go and Hanging On

Your child is walking around with new skin—tender and *very* sensitive. Unfortunately, just at the moment in her life when she needs *more* TLC, most parents tend to get heavier with their disciplinary techniques. Discipline for a teenager actually works better if you get lighter. Loosen up. Shift your position. Become an adviser or a consultant to your teenager instead of a manager.

MOM KNOWS BEST

Adolescents can be terrible to their parents. Don't take it personally. They can also be sweet, thoughtful, and supportive. *That* part you can take personally. No problem!

After all, you've been letting go since you kissed him good-bye and closed the door on his kindergarten classroom. Now it's time to let go again, to step back and give him room to grow. That's not so easy when he's still in your face. You're watching him grow and still arguing about being a little bit more considerate about people who are *sleeping* when he's making elaborate midnight snacks and clattering every pot and pan in the house.

The challenge is to hang on and stay involved even as you grant more autonomy. Your adolescent still needs guidance and support. You're letting go of your direct hands-on involvement, not your interest.

Actually, I'd Sooner Forget About It

Take a moment and think about your own adolescence. Junior high school! Was the experience: (a) positive, (b) negative, or (c) a little of both? How has your experience affected your expectations of what your child's adolescence will be like?

Parents tend to expect their children to have similar experiences to their own. The dad who was shut in lockers by peers and given wedgies in gym class will dread his son's adolescence. The mom who was popularity queen will dreamily wait for her daughter to experience the glory. The grown-up who "went wrong" and spent eighth grade smoking cigarettes and joints behind the portables will watch his budding daughter like a *hawk*.

MOM KNOWS BEST

Your child's experience of adolescence will be her own. I *know* you know this; I'm just reminding you. Remember, your memories are colored by the *hormones* you were on!

Whatever the reality turns out to be, keep reminding yourself that adolescence is not all bad. It has its moments of joy and glory, too, and these highs can be as high as the lows are low. It's a wonderful adventure watching your little baby develop into a fully-formed person.

"WHO *AM* I?"

Adolescence is when the lifelong process of self-definition really begins. It's not so much a question of figuring out what kind of job or career he'll have, though goodness knows the pressure's on these days to make career decisions early, even at the beginning of high school. No, his big task is figuring out who he is and what *kind* of person he'll be. Your adolescent may try on identities like Halloween costumes. Preppy, hip hop, biker dude—whatever the look, he's still your kid. When it's just the clothes and hair, I'd say let it slide. When behavior shifts, however, pay attention. Something else may be going on, like depression, drug use, or an improvement in attitude. Hey, it's not *always* bad news, you know! In any case, the family rules still hold. Adolescent or not, everybody has the right to a certain level of respect.

"I'm an Individual!"

As your adolescent tries on personas, he's learning to define himself by who he's *not:* You.

In early adolescence, kids feel a deep need to assert their independence and uniqueness. They often do this by trying to look exactly the same as everybody else (go figure) and taking stupid risks to prove how self-reliant they are. Many parents don't understand how important it is for a child to feel part of a group. The kid who is unable to conform will suffer. Don't push the child to be too individualistic. This is a very social stage, and it will pass; your child and her friends will stop looking like Dolly the Cloned Sheep in a couple of years. For now, bear with it. Keep fostering those other interests, and let the hairstyles and clothing fall as they may.

Don't take it personally that you're second banana right now (at least until there's a crisis). Adolescence is the era of friends. It's normal for social relationships to become at least as important as family, sometimes more so. This is part of the process your child must go through to figure out who, what, and why she is, and how she's going to spend her life.

"Mom, You're Embarrassing Me!"

Adolescents have to separate from their parents. Wouldn't it be nice if they could do it in a civilized and orderly fashion, instead of treating you like a leper? Cheer up. You'll survive the "I'm ducking down 'cause I don't want my friends to see me in this dorky car" stage and the one that follows it, the "Meet me three blocks away if you're going to wear one of your *gross* blouses" phase. The fact that your child thinks you're the squarest thing since Rubik's Cubes can be disconcerting to your cooler-than-thou ego, but try and tell yourself that this is her job. What would she turn out like if she never rebelled?

Bite Your Tongue!

Your adolescent child sees you as a real person, warts, lumps, and all. He needs to separate from you, so he focuses on your flaws. Waaahhh! You're no longer the goddess. You may feel sad at the loss of a worshiper, but remember that he feels sorrow and betrayal at the loss of a deity, too.

This is one reason why voicing disapproval doesn't work with adolescents. If you say, "Ugh! Stay away from cigarettes! Don't you know those things will kill you?" don't be surprised if she starts smoking a pack a day. If you say, "I think Amy is a bad influence on you," who do you think she'll spend time with every day? Give her room and time to reflect and make her own decisions. Trust me, your child *wants* to do right by herself.

Moodiness

Your adolescent has a lot on her mind. It's stressful growing up—school pressures, social pressures, family pressures, and a whole new body besides. Give her room for her moods, which are her way of processing. Don't ever assume that she will want to talk about something on the spur-of-the-moment, just because *you* want to. Make an appointment with your adolescent. Talk about adolescence, moodiness and all. You may both learn something. Annette sat her 14-year-old son down and said, "Look, I've never been the mother of a kid your age, and you've never been this age.

We're going to get through this together." By understanding *why* the moods are happening, you'll have an easier time not taking it so personally. You'll also be able to determine if there's something more serious going on.

I FEEL BAD SO I'M ACTING BAD

There's a dark side to adolescence for many kids. Depression and self-destructive behavior is all too common. Eating disorders, sexual misconduct, and drug abuse abound. *These* are the parts of adolescence that scare parents, give them ulcers, and make them wish for a deep freeze (insert the kid at 11 and remove at 21).

Self-Image Problems

Society is bombarded by media images of what the human body *should* look like. Our ideal woman is thin, tall, and large-breasted; men are supposed to have washboard abs and big biceps. Such cultural messages can strongly affect your adolescents, distorting their self-image and lowering their self-esteem. Unless you cancel your magazine subscriptions, go after the TV with a shotgun, build a Barbie Doll bonfire, and move yourself and your kids to a hut in the hills, it's hard to know how you can protect your kids from receiving these messages. However, you *can* help them maintain a strong self-image by giving encouragement, trust, love, limits, and consequences. An adolescent child who receives love, structure, and respect will learn to love, structure, and respect himself. Here are some ways to keep your child's self-image strong:

◆ *Model good self-imaging.* Stop carping on your own looks and failures.

◆ *Encourage your child to get involved in physical activities* that make him feel good about himself.

◆ **Never** *criticize how your child looks,* even if you think you're being constructive in your criticism. "Look at that cellulite on your thighs, Ellen. I think you should be riding your bike to school at least three times a week." Uh-uh, Mom.

Eating Disorders

Eating disorders are fairly common among teens and are related to very poor body image and stress. Eating disorders are very serious and life-threatening conditions. If your daughter (90 percent of all teenagers with eating disorders are female) is developing an eating disorder, you may be the last person to notice. No, Mom, you're not dumb. First of all, you're with your kid every day. Her loss of weight may be gradual and you may not notice. Also, bulimics are often "normal" weight. Finally, you may suffer from *parent blindness*—you don't want to believe that it's happening, so you just don't see it.

 WISE WORDS

Parent blindness is a syndrome suffered by parents who, because they love their kids and want the best for them, cannot see what's truly going on in their kids' lives.

The two most common eating disorders are *anorexia* (self-starvation because of a distorted body image) and *bulimia* (cycles of bingeing and self-induced purging). Eating disorders plague many bright, motivated girls. According to the American Anorexia/Bulimia Association, 1 percent of teenage girls in the United States suffer from anorexia; of these, up to 10 percent die from it. Eating disorders are scary. The good news is that in the last 20 or so years, awareness about these disorders has increased dramatically, as have resources for treating them. Many schools have educational programs about eating disorders, and school staff and counselors know to be on the lookout for them. If you believe your child is suffering from an eating disorder, take it seriously.

- ◆ *Get help.* You can't do this one alone. Start with the school and the doctor's office—they often have on-site resources or recommendations. Get help for yourself, too. Being the parent of a child with an eating disorder can be very stressful. You might want to consider family or individual counseling. (See Chapter 13 for more information.)

◆ *Get information.* You'll find many books on the subject at your public library. The American Anorexia/Bulimia Association, at (212) 891-8686, offers support, literature, and information about anorexia, bulimia, and other eating disorders.

◆ *Accept right now that you cannot control your child's eating.* Food is not an area you can effectively regulate. If you try to set boundaries and limits around your child's eating patterns, you may make it worse. With professional help, you may be able to help your child set her own goals and limits. You will probably fail if you try to do it on your own.

WISE WORDS

Anorexia is an eating disorder characterized by self-starvation. *Bulimia* is characterized by cycles of bingeing (overeating) and self-induced purging (vomiting).

It's a Bad Old World

Some kids are worriers—they always have been, they always will be. Often the brightest, most imaginative kids are the ones who stress out about the state of the world and the ones who are most vulnerable to depression and despair. These sensitive kids often feel alone and misunderstood, yet it's not only the worriers who are at risk—any adolescent who doesn't yet know how to handle her stress can get into self-destructive patterns: eating disorders, hurting herself, or taking unnecessary risks. It can be a very painful time of life. You can help.

◆ *Be the Big Ear.* Take time to listen, even when you don't have answers. (Nobody has answers to questions about poverty, cruelty, environmental destruction, or racism.)

◆ *Teach your child coping strategies:* taking yoga, volunteering, or getting out of that dank room and into the sun once in a while.

◆ *Get your teenager—and yourself—some outside help.* Chapter 13 tells you how to do that.

TRADING CHILDREN

Adolescence can be *way* hard. Your kid is an utter beast, and then just when you can't handle it anymore, the mom of one of his friends compliments you on what a fine, upstanding, considerate, warm, and bright citizen you've raised. "Who?" you reply, glancing behind you to see if she's addressing somebody else, somebody who doesn't have a mass of cranky hormones for a child. "Your son," she says. "Boy, I wish Sammy were so polite and kind. What a jerk he is these days." You think of her son, Sammy. Wasn't it just yesterday you were wondering why you couldn't trade in your model for one of those?

Kids rarely show their parents their gifts. Here's an idea that's actually pretty sound: If things are *very* tense in your household, consider swapping children with another parent for a while. You think I'm joking, but I'm not. It's not a vacation. You'll still be a mother caring for an adolescent. Because the kid isn't your own, however, the major tensions just won't be there. Meanwhile, removed from the usual household conflicts, your teenager will learn some flexibility and probably have a great time. Try it for a week. Some people do it for a whole semester, but that's fairly extreme. Here are some tips for trading kids:

- *Trading kids only works if* everybody *is game.* Don't railroad this through with your child—she'll think you don't want her anymore.

- *Make sure you feel comfortable with the safety level and basic values in the household your child will be spending time in.* If you don't feel your child will be safe, don't do it!

- *Make sure to spend lots of time with your child,* even if she's sleeping at somebody else's.

- *Let go!* Don't call and nag her about whether she's helping in the kitchen or burping at the dinner table. Let the other family handle it for a while. That's the point—you're *trading* kids.

- *Treat the incoming child as a member of the household*—he's not a guest. Clearly explain your expectations and family rules. Provide positive reinforcement.

◆ *Discuss discipline with the other parent in advance.* State your expectations, rules, and bottom lines. When Jane and Jim took Sammy for a week in exchange for Jonah, Jane told Sammy's parents, "I don't believe in corporal punishment. I'm fine with any kind of curfew you want to set with Jonah, but Sammy will have to follow his own conscience with us. Also, in our house, nobody smokes. Sammy will either have to quit or keep it well away from the house."

Absence makes the heart grow fonder. You'll miss your child terribly, while you find out that Sammy is no angel. A short period of physical distance may turn out to be just what the doctor ordered.

ADULT ALLIES

In Chapter 10, we talked about teachers and coaches as helpful parenting partners. Concerned adults can also make great allies and friends for your adolescent child. Did you have an old aunt you could confide in? A friend in an older age group can give your child a new perspective, one she'll never get from you, because you're Mom, with all that that entails.

If your child has an adult ally, stay out of the relationship. Treat it like any other friendship your child might have, and respect her privacy. Don't ask your child what she and her ally talk about! (You don't want to force her to lie.) And don't ever ask the adult friend to betray your child's trust, even if you're worried about the child. Get your information elsewhere. The sanctity of the friendship should not be broken.

But wait. What if your child befriends (or is befriended by) an adult you don't trust? That's a toughie. If you have reason to believe that your child's physical safety is in question, or if you sense some inappropriate sexual vibes, you can and should deal with the issue in a direct fashion and talk about it. Otherwise, bite your tongue. Remember, the fastest way to drive your adolescent deeper into a friendship is to express disapproval. Stress your values, be open for listening, and talk with your child in a way that stresses respect. Throw your trust his way and let him catch it!

BREATHE, MOST KIDS MAKE IT THROUGH

There is no growth without stress; this is a biological fact. Adolescence is a stage of life, and most kids make it through reasonably intact. They emerge on the other side as thinking, feeling people who have lived with love, loss, wonder, joy, and beauty.

Take care of yourself. If your adolescent child is like most kids her age, you can use a little extra support in your life. This goes double if she's unhappy or depressed. Letting go is partly for your child's sake and partly for your own. As your teen begins to bumble her way into her own life, make sure that she isn't taking you along with her. You don't want to be left in the lurch, empty and bereft, when she leaves home in a few years.

THE LEAST YOU NEED TO KNOW

- ◆ It's the adolescent's job to separate, and it's your job to remain sane while she does it.

- ◆ Shift your approach from concerned and hands-on to concerned and hands-off.

- ◆ Adolescence can be enjoyed, not just feared.

- ◆ An adolescent child who receives love, structure, and respect will learn to love, structure, and respect himself.

- ◆ In despair? Try trading children with another parent for a while.

- ◆ Breathe easy. Adolescence is a flowering, and most kids make it through.

Sex, Drugs, and How to Talk About Them

In This Chapter

◆ Sex, drugs, and discipline

◆ Living with raging hormones (not yours!)

◆ Finding the facts on drug and alcohol use, misuse, and abuse

◆ What to say about your own sordid past

Blink and your baby is a child. Blink again and you've got a pre-adolescent. Life is spinning faster and faster—either that or you're getting older and older. Your child will be a full-fledged teenager before you can say, "hippity hop to the candy shop." Sleepless nights. You toss and turn, worrying about your not-so-little one who's starting to go to parties. Have you told him enough about alcohol and drugs? Is he going to become sexually active soon? What should you say—or not say—about danger, disease, addiction, desire, and hormones?

KEEPING YOUR KIDS SAFE, HAPPY, AND HEALTHY

Now, more than ever, you need to *hang* with your kids. You need to keep talking, to keep the warmth and love flowing. It's never too early to prepare for—and talk about—sex, alcohol, and drugs. But how do you do it? What do you say?

Since you can't talk about what you don't know, this chapter will give you a brief rundown on some of the issues and facts. The next chapter (Chapter 13) is full of resource listings. Talking with your kids about sex, alcohol, and drugs is scary for many parents. It always helps to have references to call on.

What do sex, alcohol, and drugs have to do with discipline? Your children need to be prepared with the knowledge and strength to make strong, healthy decisions, to have the inner boundaries to say no when they're not ready for sex, alcohol, or drugs. How do they get these inner boundaries? They internalize the discipline they've been taught. *That's* the connection.

OH, THOSE RAGING HORMONES!

Children are reaching puberty younger and younger. According to figures in the book *Raising a Daughter,* by Don Elium and Jeanne Elium, the average age that a girl begins menstruation has plunged in the last 100 years from 16 to 12.8 years. The reasons for this biological shift are not completely clear. Whatever the reasons, it's clear that kids are maturing physically at younger ages, and that means...hormones!

The Center for Population Options estimates that 25 percent of 15-year-old girls and 33 percent of 15-year-old boys have had intercourse. Fifteen years old? That's not so far off, is it Mom? Sexual desire is a wonderful thing—I believe it's one of the joys and wonders of being human—but it's pretty strong medicine. It's hard for kids to know what to do with it.

It's *never* too early to start talking about sex—and listening. Basic facts about sex can be transmitted as soon as the questions about bodies and how they work begin—as young as three or four. If you handle questions about sexuality casually as they come up, you'll avoid the palm-sweating-uncomfortable "birds and bees" talk with your preadolescent. By that time he'll already know the facts, or he'll think he knows.

Eeeuu! Yuck! That's What Those Bees Do?

The school-age years, ages 7 through 11, are often referred to as the *latency* period, where sexual interest is muted. Listen in on the whispers at a 9-, 10-, or 11-year-old's slumber party, though, and you might get a different impression. What do those muffled giggles turn out to be about? Dirty jokes, naturally. Kids know they're not supposed to be interested in sex. They're also deeply curious and nervous about it, and no wonder. Commercials, movies, magazines, TV shows, billboards—everywhere they look, the message is sex, sex, sex!

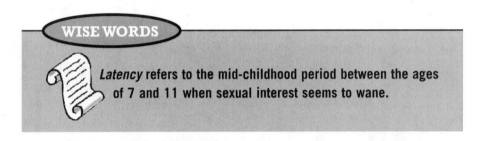

WISE WORDS

Latency refers to the mid-childhood period between the ages of 7 and 11 when sexual interest seems to wane.

Whatcha Gonna Do About It?

Simple. Talk about it. Children need to have support for their growing sexuality. Even if you ignore it, it won't go away. And get your head out of the sand, Mama Ostrich, the evidence is in—education helps. The World Health Organization sees a direct link between when sex education begins and a delay in the beginning of sexual activity. They've also found that sex education leads to a decrease in overall sexual activity and an increase in *safer sex* practices.

Sex education, like discipline, is a *process,* not a one-time, sit-down-and-blurt-the-facts-out thing. Most parents feel uncomfortable talking about sex, not just you. I'm sorry, but you're going to have to grit your teeth and do it anyway. Don't worry about putting ideas into your child's head. Junior or Juniorina is like the rest of the human race—wired for reproduction. Draw pictures, read books together, but give the cold, hard facts about sex. And it's not just a matter of letting the school handle the education. They can help, but ultimately it's your responsibility, and unfortunately, all too many school districts provide inadequate programs.

For help and resources on talking to your child about sexuality and birth control, contact the Planned Parenthood Federation of

America. Look in your phone book for a local clinic, contact the main office at 810 Seventh Avenue, New York, NY 10019, (212) 541-7800, or call (800) 230-7526 to be transferred to the clinic nearest you.

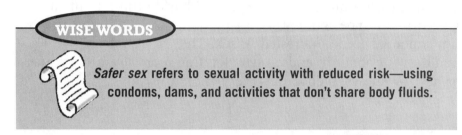

WISE WORDS

Safer sex refers to sexual activity with reduced risk—using condoms, dams, and activities that don't share body fluids.

The most important thing, when you're talking about sex, is to be real. Don't idealize it with romantic notions or platitudes, and don't try to scare the bejeebers out of the poor child. You can and should express your values, wherever they fall along the continuum (from "Wait until marriage" to "I think it's important for people to experiment before they settle down"), but don't lecture. Keep the statements statements, and concentrate on transmitting the facts. Let your child know that no matter what, you're there for her.

Homosexuality

Since up to 10 percent of the population has a same-sex sexual orientation (gay, lesbian, or bisexual), it's vital to talk about this issue with your kids. Homosexuality appears randomly throughout the population. Talking about it in a straightforward way should be part of the sex education process *whether or not* you think your child might be gay or lesbian. You're raising a respectful child here; let her know that homosexuality is just another form of diversity. Homosexuality can't be prevented or "cured." What most gays and lesbians want is what all people want: love, respect, and acceptance.

And by the way, Mom, there are *no* clear signs of what your child's orientation is or will be. It's not unusual, for instance, for sex play and experimentation to happen between members of the same sex, as well as the opposite sex, regardless of sexual orientation. It's normal for kids to experiment and explore.

You don't know what your kid's orientation will turn out to be, but your kid might. Many kids are aware of their sexual orientation very young, and the burden for gay and bi-sexual kids can be almost too much to handle. Despite some progress in recent years, society is still deeply homophobic. It's no wonder gay and lesbian youth are far more likely than other teenagers to attempt suicide. According to the Center for Population Options, they may make up 30 percent of suicides among youth annually. Be the kind of parent a kid can talk to about anything.

If your child is gay and you need more information or support, contact PFLAG (Parents, Families, and Friends of Lesbians and Gays). This organization has chapters and support groups across the country. Call its central office in Washington, D.C., at (202) 638-4200 for information about its quarterly publication and reports, as well as referrals to chapters and youth programs near you.

AIDS and Other Sexually Transmitted Diseases

Sex is dangerous for this generation. Kids know it. They know HIV/AIDS kills and that diseases like herpes are currently incurable. Guess what: Many are having sex anyway. Slogans about "safe sex" don't make much of an impression when you're a teenager. Most of us, at that age, believe on some level that we're going to live forever, even though we really "know" better.

Don't flip out. Maybe your kid will, maybe he won't—yet. Your best bet is to teach him about *safer sex* while not lecturing too much. Be specific about what he can do to make sex safer, and where he can go for help.

Ignorance can be death, and many schools are still giving out inadequate information. If you—or your kids—have questions about HIV and AIDS, call the Centers for Disease Control National AIDS Hotline at (800) 342-AIDS. They are open 24 hours, you (or your child) will be completely anonymous, the call is free, and they can also provide you with written information and referrals to resource centers near you.

MOM ALWAYS SAID

"Safer sex" is indeed safer, but no sexual intercourse is completely free of the risk of sexually transmitted diseases.

Pregnancy

AIDS and other STDs are *way* scary, but don't forget about a problem that's been around even longer—traditional, old-fashioned pregnancy. The Center for Population Options has estimated that only 66 percent of teenage women use a contraceptive the first time they have intercourse, 50 percent of premarital teen pregnancies occur within six months of first intercourse, and one in five teenage women who are sexually active become pregnant.

What's the answer? Birth control. When it's done in a caring fashion and backed up by plenty of conversation and information, supplying a teenager with birth control is a safe and sensible thing to do. *But doesn't that just encourage sexual activity?* I hear moms all over the planet protesting. Actually, no—no more than stocking the bathroom cabinet with bandages encourages your child to go out and cut himself.

A girl should have her first gynecological exam when she begins menstruation. Every child of 11 or older, regardless of gender, should understand the human male and female reproductive systems and know how to prevent pregnancy. There are some lessons you don't want your kids to learn the hard way.

Becoming an "Askable" Adult

I know, you're still feeling squeamish. Your kids will sense that. (They're like wild animals, they *smell* your fear!) If you want your child to tell you "wassup," or ask questions about sex, drugs, and alcohol, you're going to have to gain (or regain) her trust. If the questions arise at a time when you don't feel comfortable answering, make an appointment with your child. Practice your poker face. When she starts "confessing," say, "Tell me more." Continue until she's talked out. *Then* you can respond. (Try a little dose of active listening.) Never get angry at her for telling the truth. If she tells you something you don't approve of, don't react in a negative way at all. You can scream later, when she's out of earshot.

EGAD, THEY'RE *FOOLING AROUND!*

What do you do when you find out your child is "fooling around"? Kissing, petting, "doing it"? There are physical and emotional risks to sex. The emotional risks you don't have a lot of say about. With work, not to mention motherly love, you may be privy to his heart-breaks and obsessions, but ultimately it's up to your teen to decide on his level of sexual involvement, unless you're planning on locking him up until he's of legal age. Instead, concentrate on helping to keep your child physically safe. Try to determine whether:

◆ There is mutual consent. Is one partner pressuring the other? Is there peer pressure to be sexually active?

◆ These are peers. Are they roughly the same age? Most pregnant teens are impregnated by much older boys or men.

◆ He or she is safe—from pregnancy, sexually transmitted diseases, and violence.

If you're able to discuss these issues *with* your child and determine the answers together, the fog of hormones might clear enough to allow your child to make safe, healthy choices.

Sexual Misbehavior

Should I curfew my child? That's a question many moms (and dads) ask. You could, but it might not make a difference. The hours between 3 and 6 P.M. are when most kids get "into trouble," and there's nothing new about that. Peggy, a woman in her 70s, tells the story of growing up in Salt Lake City, Utah. Unlike the other young girls her age, she never had a curfew. "I figure you can get pregnant just as easily before 9 P.M. as you can afterward," her father told her. Peggy, who survived adolescence before Mom was even born, chuckles and shakes her head, "That damn man put me on the *honor* system!"

Sexual misbehavior is common among young adolescents. Handle it like any other misbehavior: Look for the positive intent, figure out the needs, and apply appropriate consequences.

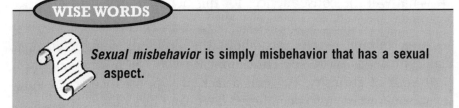

WISE WORDS

Sexual misbehavior is simply misbehavior that has a sexual aspect.

Here's a scenario: Last month, 13-year-old Tom was caught making calls to phone sex services. Tom acted repentant and promised he'd never do it again. Then the phone bill came, and there was $279 of charges to 900 numbers.

Some possible reactions:

♦ You flip out. Your sweet son is a sex maniac! Not to mention all that money! You scream at him until he cringes, and then you storm out of the room. The shamed and guilty look on his face haunts you.

♦ You remain silent. You buy him a stack of girlie magazines and a dozen condoms, and you leave them on his bed. You have a 900 number block put on your phone, and you plead with the phone company to remove the charges.

♦ You approach Tom, phone bill in hand, and say, "Honey, we got the phone bill today. We have to talk. Can I make an appointment with you for after dinner tonight?"

If you picked the last reaction, your mom instincts are right on target. (Though this one might best be handled by a father or father figure.) But now, all too soon, "after dinner" comes around. Yikes! It's time to talk! What the heck are you going to say?

In the first place, you're going to use active and proactive listening (see Chapter 5):

♦ Try to determine Tom's positive intent. What was going on emotionally with Tom when he made those calls? Was it lust? Frustration? Loneliness? Self-destructiveness (knowing he'd get caught)? Were the calls fun?

♦ What's been happening recently, with Tom and with you?

♦ What is it that Tom needs?

♦ What is it that *you* need?

♦ What will the consequences for this behavior be?

After talking extensively about the problem, you determine that Tom needs more sex education. He was calling the sex lines partly out of curiosity. He feels a lack of support for his growing sexuality. Tom has also been bored lately and he's having trouble in his social life and in his relationships with other kids. For your part, you're getting the feeling that he needs more supervision.

As a consequence, you agree to pay the phone charges—for now—and block 900 number access. Tom will work off his debt to you by helping you paint the house on weekends. To deal with his loneliness and boredom, you'll call about a summer science camp he's been interested in. You encourage him to have friends over more often because you realize he needs more of a social life. And, since he knows the sex education basics, is hopelessly curious, but isn't ready for sex himself, you encourage him to read more literature with sexual content—maybe even the *good* stuff, like D.H. Lawrence, Nabokov, and Anais Nin. He's old enough, he's curious, and it will give him an education in more ways than one!

DRUGS AND ALCOHOL: HYSTERIA DOESN'T HELP

Face it, kids are exposed to drugs from a young age. It doesn't matter where you move—the most pristine mountain community or the inner city. One reason kids experiment with drugs is because they're available. Here are the scary realities: Cigarette smoking is on the rise again; alcohol abuse is rampant. It's not going to go away; people have always experimented with mind-altering chemicals. Your household is not immune to the dangers. So, Mama, how are you gonna cope?

Getting hysterical won't help your child learn to make safe, healthy choices. Lecturing won't help either; if a child is told "Just Say No" too many times, she's likely to want to do the opposite. Most kids will want to experiment with drugs and alcohol at some point in the future. Your job as Mom is to be candid and educate them about what lies ahead.

ALL IN THE FAMILY

In a 1993 survey, University of Michigan researchers found that 26.2 percent of eighth graders surveyed had used alcohol in the previous 30 days. Seven and eight-tenths percent had been drunk, 16.7 percent had smoked cigarettes, and 5.1 percent had used marijuana. Between eighth and tenth grades, those numbers jumped significantly.

What Keeps Your Child Safe?

A child with a sense of his own strengths (and weaknesses) is less likely to have problems, including problems with drug and alcohol abuse. Using positive discipline and reinforcement will help your child respect his body, feel confident, feel lovable enough to resist peer pressure, and develop a set of goals.

Why Do Kids Use Drugs?

Look, nobody would use drugs if they made you feel *awful*. Why do *you* use drugs? Caffeine, nicotine, alcohol, Prozac, Acetaminophen, cocaine, chocolate, marijuana—the standard definition of a drug is any substance that can produce physical, emotional, or mental changes in people. How many drugs do *you* use, and what kind of behavior are you modeling?

Now—and here's the part that makes a lot of parents cringe—what about in high school? Junior high school? Do you have fond (or not so fond) memories of worshiping the porcelain deity after sneaking into your parents' liquor cabinet? Do you want your kid to follow in your footsteps? (I doubt it.) Did your parents have any control over you?

Kids use drugs and alcohol for many of the reasons adults do: Drugs make them feel good, give them a built-in social scene, help them feel less self-conscious, and relieve stress and boredom.

"Mom! I'm Shocked!"

Hey, I didn't say using drugs or alcohol was a *good* thing. An adult deciding to have a couple of glasses of wine in the evening with friends and getting a little relaxed and loopy is *not* the same as a bunch of 12-year-olds puffing a joint in the bathroom at school.

Drugs affect concentration, mood, and thinking functions. They can disrupt the learning process. Some are extremely addictive. Many affect health. Kids who use alcohol and drugs may have trouble setting limits and boundaries, particularly around sex. They are distorting their reality just at the time that they are working out their identity ("Who am I anyway?"). And like adults, some can use drugs casually or socially without serious consequences, while others have addictive personalities.

ALL IN THE FAMILY

Nancy Rubin, long-term social living teacher and author of *Ask Me If I Care*, a *great* resource book for any parent dealing with sex, drugs, and alcohol issues, suggests changing "Just Say No" to "Just Say Know."

I know, you're getting those quivers in your tummy again. "My stress levels are rising, Mom!" Here's what to do about it:

◆ *Educate yourself.* Not all drugs are the same. The dangers of tobacco are different from the dangers of marijuana, and the dangers of marijuana are different from the dangers of pre-scribed medicines, cocaine/crack, heroine, speed, XTC, PCP, LSD, and so on. You do yourself and your child a disservice when you lump them together. Find out what each drug is and what its effects, dangers, and addiction rates are. Try the local library.

◆ *Model a good relationship with alcohol and drugs.* If you're a habitu-al user, your child is *far* more likely to have problems with drugs. According to Darryl S. Inaba and William E. Cohen, authors of *Uppers, Downers, and All Arounders: Physical and Mental Effects of Psychoactive Drugs,* if one parent is an alcoholic or an addict, the child is 34 percent more likely to become an alco-holic or suffer from a drug addiction than a child whose parent is not an alcoholic or addict. If both parents suffer from alco-holism or addiction, the child is 400 percent more likely. Twenty-eight million Americans have at least one alcoholic or drug-addicted parent. The resource listings in Chapter 13 are for you, too, Mom.

◆ *Provide clear guidelines, limits, and consequences for misbehavior.* Figure out what you expect from your Reasonable Child, and let him know those expectations. Expect that he may slip up occasionally, and keep talking about it.

What About Legal Drugs?

It's legal, does that make it better? Let's look at the numbers. According to Nancy Rubin, author of *Ask Me If I Care: Voices from an*

American High School, well over 500,000 deaths every year are directly attributed to alcohol and tobacco. Only 5,000 to 6,000 deaths are attributed to cocaine, crack, and heroine annually, and none are directly attributed to marijuana use.

In fact, if you want to know what keeps me awake at night, it's nicotine. A lot of people think marijuana is the "gateway" drug, the drug most likely to lead to experimentation with other drugs. Actually, that dubious honor may go to tobacco, which also happens to be the most addicting drug of all. According to the American Cancer Society, 40 percent of all grade-school children experiment with smoking, and the younger a child starts smoking, the harder it is to quit later in life. More than one million teenagers in the United States become regular smokers annually.

ALL IN THE FAMILY

 Several factors determine what becomes the "gateway" drug for a particular individual: availability, cost (hey, crack is cheap!), what and how drugs are depicted in the media, and the home attitudes toward—and exposure to—smoking, drinking, or a particular drug.

This doesn't mean that smoking marijuana is great for you. It affects short-term memory, can impair judgment and coordination, and leads to lethargy. And anyway, it's *never* healthy to get smoke in your lungs. But let's get our anxieties in perspective.

Drug Use, Misuse, Abuse

Not all drug and alcohol use is the same. Inaba and Cohen list five general stages of drug use, commenting that many people never get past stages one or two. The five stages are experimental, social, habitual, abuse, and addiction. The speed of a person's path through these stages is largely based on biological predisposition. Someone with a family history of alcoholism or drug abuse may move from the experimental stage to addiction very quickly, while a child with no history of abuse in her family may experiment a few times and stop, or casually use drugs or alcohol for years before becoming habituated and eventually addicted.

The Bugaboo of Peer Pressure

It's a cop-out to tell your kid "Just Say No" and leave it at that. The peer pressures a child faces are not necessarily direct. ("What are you, chicken? Just one little hit....") Usually they are more subtle. Alcohol and drug use is a social thing, and friendship is built on shared experiences. If your child opts out, she may find herself losing friends, not because they don't like her or respect her decision but because of the loss of shared experiences. The child who resists social pressure to use drugs or alcohol needs extra support as she goes through what might be a period of mourning.

Telling Your Kids About Your Sordid Past

Are you gonna tell? Many parents are afraid that if they tell their kids just how *much* sex, drugs, and alcohol they indulged in when they were young, they'll set a bad example and won't have a moral leg to stand on when their kids decide to experiment on their own. Other parents believe that it would be dishonest to lie, even when they don't want their own kids to experiment. I believe in honesty, but not the kind of honesty that means waxing eloquent about the time you and Jimmy dropped acid and had unprotected sex down by the old water tank in tenth grade. Keep your dignity, and your stories. But answer honestly when asked. When you talk with your child about sex, drugs, and alcohol:

◆ Express your opinions about use, misuse, and experimentation, and don't omit your own learning experiences. They matter.

◆ No ranting, no raving.

◆ These are important issues. Show that they do matter to you. Don't ignore them.

◆ Never use the "Don't do what I did" or the "Drugs are stronger these days and the social scene has changed" rap. It will probably piss your kid off, and it won't work.

Getting Help

Substance use can easily turn into abuse. Sometimes you, the mom, are the last to know. If you're unsure about how your kid is doing—in any way, not just with drugs—try talking to her teachers at school. Don't ask directly about drugs, just call up for a general chat. If the teachers have noticed anything troubling, they should let you know. Chapter 13 has some suggestions for how to find help, whether for your child or for yourself.

MOM KNOWS BEST

Establish ongoing contact with your child's teachers and school. Then, if your child begins to have trouble with sex, alcohol, or drugs, you'll have already built a relationship of trust.

THE LEAST YOU NEED TO KNOW

- ◆ Sex education helps reduce early sexual activity, and it's *your* responsibility.

- ◆ Treat sexual misbehavior as you would any other form of misbehavior.

- ◆ Your kids *will* be exposed to alcohol and drugs, and they may experiment.

- ◆ It's "Just Say Know," not "Just Say No."

Big Trouble

You're in it up to your neck, and the water is scalding. Trouble! With-a-capital-T-that-rhymes-with-C-that-stands-for-Child. Sometimes, no matter what you do, your kid continues to act out, rebel, skip school, swear, lie, do drugs or alcohol, and, when confronted, refuse to change her behavior. Have you grown a bad seed? Not necessarily. This is a chapter about big trouble—what signs to look for and what steps to take when you can't fix it yourself, when you're at your wit's end.

WHEN PREVENTION DOESN'T WORK

Your household is filled with nastiness, lies, moodiness, dropping grades, slovenly behavior, and retreat from the world, all in the form of your own precious child. You've gone through the "It's a phase" phase, but it's gotta be more than that—none of the other kids in your child's class are quite *this* incorrigible. Or she's depressed, self-destructive, losing too much weight, and exercising frantically. Perhaps he's disruptive, distractible, and explosive. Whatever it is, you're staring at the ceiling at 3 A.M. (again!), and the cold, hard truth finally sinks in: Your kid is in trouble. Okay, stop beating yourself up, Mom, there's no time for that now. The boat is sinking. It's time for Reasonable Mom to take charge.

MOM KNOWS BEST

Sometimes it's hard to admit that your kid is having big trouble. This is human. It's for *you* that the self-actualization movement created the slogan, *Denial is not a river in Egypt.*

COULD IT BE BIOLOGICAL?—ADD AND ADHD

You've done it all—consistency, limits, consequences, and lots of affection, attention, and love. You've done good parenting. Yet your kid is volatile, not doing well in school, disruptive, unhappy, easily distracted, obsessive, and generally unpleasant to be around. Could it be biological?

Attention Deficit Disorder (ADD) and *Attention Deficit Hyperactive Disorder (ADHD)* are the most commonly diagnosed psychiatric illnesses among children. It's estimated that up to 10 percent of all school-age children are currently on medication for these disorders. ADD and ADHD are biological—they are inborn traits. (So stop *blaming* yourself, okay?)

Since so much of discipline is the art of paying attention, discipline can be a real challenge for a child—and the family of a child—who has an attention deficit. Kids with ADD/ADHD are at high risk for developing learning disorders and behavioral difficulties.

WISE WORDS

Attention Deficit Disorder is a biochemical disorder in the orbital-frontal cortex of the brain, causing inattention, impulsiveness, hyperactivity, and distractibility.

Signs and Symptoms

ADD and ADHD are characterized by inattention, impulsiveness, hyperactivity, difficulty with prioritizing, the tendency to get lost in fantasy, and distractibility. Of course, all people show these behaviors from time to time. The difference is that children with ADD/ADHD show them frequently, for a greater duration, and cannot control them.

Diagnosing ADD/ADHD is not easy, and it's not a do-it-yourself activity. High-energy kids are sometimes mistakenly called "hyper," when really they just have more energy than their old, sleep-deprived parents. Don't type your child.

ADD/ADHD kids are easily overwhelmed by stimuli. They *intend* to finish what they begin, but they're so easily distracted that tasks often get away from them. They need careful direction and strong limits.

Much of your child's eventual success will depend on how her ADD/ADHD is handled. ADD/ADHD *can* lead to learning challenges and lowered self-respect. Kids with these disorders feel they can't *do* things, that they're stupid, or that they're forever getting into trouble, yet many, many productive and brilliant citizens, and a tremendous number of artists and highly creative people, have ADD/ADHD. Most have average or above-average intelligence.

"What Can I Do?"

◆ *Get a proper diagnosis.* For many, symptoms of this inborn disability don't become severe until middle or older childhood. Some kids are diagnosed much younger.

◆ *Read, read, talk to other parents, and read.* There's a wide selection of books out now on ADD/ADHD. Check the bibliography in the back of this book.

◆ *Contact CHADD* (Children and Adults with Attention Deficit Disorders), 499 N.W. 70th Avenue, Suite 101, Plantation, FL 33317, (800) 233-4050. CHADD is a nonprofit organization with 650 branches worldwide. Most of the people who staff CHADD are either ADD adults or parents of kids with ADD, so they'll know what's going on with you. CHADD publishes (among other things) *Attention!,* a magazine designed for parents of children with ADD or ADHD.

◆ *Don't leap to drug therapy—get a second opinion.* Talk to other ADD/ADHD parents.

Providing a Nourishing Home

Kids with ADD/ADHD need a lot of structure and limits in their lives. Education—for yourself, your child, your parents, and your child's teacher—can be incredibly helpful. Kids can learn to complete tasks one by one using lists, regular routines, and a simpler lifestyle with less distraction. Here are some "beginning" tips for dealing with your child's ADD or ADHD:

◆ *Keep your instructions short and simple.* ADD/ADHD kids have trouble remembering sequences.

◆ *Be consistent* with responses and consequences.

◆ *Work on the relaxation thing.* Release that stress.

◆ *Get counseling for your child and for yourself.* ADD/ADHD can be extremely stressful on a family, especially when undiagnosed. Counseling should be linked with other ADD/ADHD therapy; just talking about it won't help.

Drug Therapy

Doctors prescribe drug therapy for many kids with ADD or ADHD. Now, Mom is not a doctor, so what I say here should be taken with a handful of grains of salt. Anecdotally, I've found that drug therapy for ADD/ADHD is a mixed bag—effective for some kids, an abject failure for others. But hey, I don't know your kid or your situation.

Ritalin is the most commonly prescribed drug for ADD/ADHD, followed by Dexedrine and Cylert. "Dexedrine?" I hear you cry. "Isn't that 'speed'?" Actually, all these drugs are "uppers," but that's not the effect they have on the brain of an ADD/ADHD person, which is somehow wired a bit differently. (Doctors aren't sure how.) What such drugs do for people with ADD/ADHD is help organize the brain, making it easier to focus and pay attention.

ALL IN THE FAMILY

Dyslexia and Dysgraphia are two other "wiring" disorders that cause learning disabilities—and great distress if undiagnosed. For information and support, contact the International Dyslexia Association (formally the Orton Dyslexia Society) at (800) ABC-D123, (410) 296-0232, or online at http://www.interdys.org. Also call the National Center for Learning Disabilities at (212) 545-7510.

SELF-ABUSE AND ADDICTION

Life for older children is increasingly stressful. When stress and depression turn inward, kids often begin to injure themselves through self-abuse (I'm not talking masturbation, here) and addictions.

◆ Self-abuse can include cutting, burning, extreme risk-taking, and other self-destructive behavior. This may be hidden behavior, or it may be fairly evident. When your 11-year-old comes home with pierced eyebrows, it may be more than just a fashion statement. Is she celebrating pain? While minor risk-taking seems to be a symptom of youth, major self-abuse requires an outside eye and possibly therapy.

◆ For eating disorders, discussed in Chapter 11, contact: The American Anorexia/Bulimia Association at (212) 891-8686.

◆ Addictions are the final step on the drug use continuum (see Chapter 12). By the time a child is addicted to a substance, there are usually a lot of other visible troubles. Problems *leak.*

Drug and alcohol addiction is a toughie. Here are some places to go for help:

Alanon-Alateen Information Service
(800) 344-2666

Alcoholics Anonymous
Look in your local phone book or write for referrals to local chapters:
General Service Office
Grand Central Station
P.O. Box 459
New York, NY 10163

Marijuana Anonymous World Services
(800) 766-6779

Nar-Anon Family Groups World Service Office
(310) 547-5800

Narcotics Anonymous World Service Office
(818) 773-9999

National Clearinghouse for Alcohol and Drug Information
(301) 468-2600

National Drug and Alcohol Treatment Referral Hotline
(800) 662-HELP

MOM KNOWS BEST

Therapy doesn't mean your child is evil or nuts, or that you are. It isn't punishment; it's a tool for healing, learning, and self-nurture.

SERIOUS MISBEHAVIORS

What do you do if things get completely out of hand? There's no way I can tell you what to do about a particular problem your child is having with serious or illegal behavior. Here, though, are some approaches to consider.

Busted!

It's every mom's nightmare: You get a call from the police station or the juvenile authorities. Your child has been hauled in for breaking the law. The first thing to do when you get that awful call is *not react.* Don't race to the car. Don't start to scream. Don't frantically call the bail bondsman. Get the facts, bite your tongue as you listen, and then get off the phone and set the timer for 15 minutes. You need that time to get it together and figure out your approach. Here are some things to try to remember when your child is arrested or in trouble with "the law":

◆ Remember that you are your child's ally. That means you are on your child's side. It does *not* mean your child is always right, or that you are your child's apologist.

◆ Remember that your child is innocent until proven guilty.

◆ Parents usually fall between two extremes: the "Let 'em rot in jail" camp and the "Oh, poor baby, let me bail you out" camp. What is your instinct now?

◆ Consider the natural consequences and whether they are appropriate or too extreme. If your kid is arrested for shoplifting a portable CD player and you don't bail her out, the authorities might keep her overnight. Will this teach her a lesson? For a sheltered nine-year-old, leaving her overnight in juvenile hall with fairly hardened reform-school kids might be more devastating than useful.

◆ Separate your anger at your child ('cause you're gonna be teed-off) from your decision about what action or approach to take.

◆ Once you decide what to do, act calmly.

A lot of moms ask, "How do I face my child?" When your child is accused of doing something seriously wrong, you'll probably be a bubbling lava pit of emotions. He's still your kid, still your sweet pookie, but the shame and anger you feel may make it hard to see that. That's normal. Resist the impulse to strangle the kid. Two wrongs make a *long* prison term. When you get time alone with your child, practice active and proactive listening to get the story. They'll help build empathy—in you—and give you an opportunity to clear your head.

If You Catch Your Child

What if you catch your child committing a serious wrong, but the authorities do not? You've got a problem here, Mom; what are you going to do about it?

- ◆ You cannot condone illegal behavior. Express your horror, shock, dismay, and disapproval immediately, but don't rant and rave.

- ◆ Stop the activity immediately.

- ◆ Get the child to a neutral place and allow some cool-down time.

- ◆ Your child will need to make restitution. How you decide to bring that about will depend upon the activity.

- ◆ Take some time to weigh what the consequences should be, and don't leap to action. Some people believe in "scaring" a kid straight. Others are concerned—and rightly so—that if they turn their child in, the ramifications will echo for a long time, possibly forever.

- ◆ When your child is in trouble, it's time to look at your own discipline. What are you modeling?

Responding to Criminal Behavior

If your child has had a criminal incident or incidents:

- ◆ Show love, love, love…and no tolerance.

- ◆ Let her know that her behavior is not morally acceptable to you. Do it quickly and cleanly and do not lecture.

- ◆ Raging won't help.

- ◆ Resist the urge to "get tough" with your child.

◆ Don't wait for it to get better or for the "phase" to pass.

◆ Remember that your child is probably feeling ashamed.

◆ Add something positive to his life—art, music, sports, or the outdoors.

The Long-Term Ramifications

After you get done dealing with the primary situation (howling at the moon, going down to the police station, arranging for legal representation, or taking a sullen, shamed kid home), you'll want to assess just how much trouble your child is in, generally.

◆ *Is this a one-time incident?* A one-time incident can be extremely worrisome. But real, long-term, serious trouble is indicated when a child gets into legal trouble more than a couple of times a year. (I'd include crimes at school, as well.)

◆ *How old is your child?* The younger the child, the more worrisome serious misbehavior is. The younger a child starts criminal patterns, for example, the harder it is to break them.

◆ *How serious is the crime?* Grand larceny or petty theft? Minor vandalism or arson? Fighting in the school yard or aggravated assault? Of course, the more extreme the behavior, the more outside help is indicated.

◆ *Assess the whole child.* Is the behavior echoed in your child's current temperament? Is she generally showing defiant or impulsive behavior? How are her relationships with her friends? How are her grades?

MOM KNOWS BEST

New evidence shows most boys in gangs don't have fathers in their lives. Whether you've got trouble or not, a positive father figure (uncle, trusted friend, counselor, "Big Brother," coach) can make a big difference to a kid.

THE VIOLENT CHILD

You only have to think of some of our current Hollywood heroes (Arnold Schwarznegger?!) to realize how close violence is to the surface of our supposedly peaceful society. Boys especially often gain status and peer respect by turning violent. If you want to reduce the violent tendencies within your child, you need to reduce his exposure to outside violence and certainly any violence within your household.

If you're in the tightening spiral of fighting violence with violence, I'd suggest you get some help to snap those patterns and start anew. Call the National Domestic Violence Hotline at (800) 799-SAFE. The TDD/TTY number is (800) 787-3224. They are available to help you 24 hours a day.

Reducing Violent Influences

There's a wide world of violence out there, and you've invited it into your house through the TV. Experts estimate that the average American kid watches six hours of TV a day and sees 11,000 murders by the time she's 14. Too much TV not only desensitizes kids to violence, it causes children to *become* more violent. Consider turning it *off* more often.

GETTING THERAPEUTIC HELP

When do you step in? When are you considered overbearing? The general rule is that you need help when somebody's (anybody's) health and safety are threatened and you're powerless to do anything about it. Believe me, assessing the situation is the hardest part. Once you've made the decision to get some help, you'll find that there are lots of resources available.

Having decided to get help for your child, be firm: This is a non-negotiable issue. Allow him to choose (or approve) whom he sees—after all, therapy creates a very personal relationship between the therapist and the client—but do *not* allow him to weasel out of going.

Where to Begin the Search

How do you find Mr. or Ms. Right? Here are some suggestions for finding a therapist or psychiatrist:

◆ *Other parents nearby.* No matter what the problem, I guarantee that your child is not alone. Are there other children struggling with similar issues in your community? Chat with their parents. Get referrals and counter-referrals. ("Don't *ever* go to Doctor Jones. That pompous creep overmedicated our Johnny.")

◆ *Other parents far away.* If you're connected to the Internet, do a little surfing, dude, and see what you come up with. There are chat groups, USENET groups, and Web pages for just about everything that exists.

◆ *School can be an excellent resource.* It may have listings or put you in touch with social service agencies that can help you find what—and who—you'll need.

◆ *Shop around.* Try a few people. Take your child for a trial session and see what he thinks and feels.

MOM KNOWS BEST

 Finding the *right* therapist matters. Get instinctual—a million diplomas can't assure empathy, insight, and wisdom. Try a session. Does this feel like a person you can trust?

M.D., Ph.D., M.F.C.C., L.C.S.W....

Alphabet soup! Mental health professionals have a confusing set of licensing regulations and initials. More important than the specific training (or which diplomas line the office walls) is the therapist herself. But if you want to know more, here's a brief breakdown of what those initials mean:

The Degree

WHAT THE DEGREE ENTAILS

M.D.   A medical doctor who may, or may not, specialize in psychological treatment (a psychiatrist). If drug treatment is indicated (antidepressants, Prozac, Ritalin, and so on), only an M.D. can prescribe them, no matter what other type of mental health professional is the primary caregiver.

Ph.D.   The other kind of doctor; she'll generally hold a Ph.D. in psychology.

M.F.C.C. Stands for Marriage, Family, and Child Counselor. The M.F.C.C. can only work with issues related to marriage, family, and children.

L.C.S.W. Licensed Clinical Social Worker.

Intern   This term can apply to trainees of several different disciplines. There are social work interns, psychology interns, medical interns, and so on.

Shopping for Therapy

It's not just what kind of mental health professional you choose, it's the format of the therapy. Some people respond best to a group dynamic, some to individual therapy. Very often, effective therapy with troubled kids involves a parental component—that means *you* get your head shrunk, too, Mom. As you begin the process of finding the *right* therapist, remain open to format suggestions. You may not know what you need.

When you first call or meet mental health professionals, quiz 'em! You're hiring them, right? This is their job interview. Here are some sample questions:

◆ Describe your training and experience.

◆ What are your rates, and how often will you meet with my child (with us)?

◆ How will you evaluate my child's (or my family's) problems?

◆ How do you approach _____ (the problem you're seeking help for)?

◆ How long does this kind of therapy last? (Keep in mind that a good therapist won't or can't say exactly how long therapy will last or how often the sessions will be until he can carefully evaluate what's going on. Be wary of a therapist who gives too quick of a response.)

◆ Will the entire family be involved? Just the child? The child and the parents?

Listen to *how* the therapist answers the questions as well as *what* she answers. Does she act as if these questions are none of your business? Does she try to brush you off? You're listening for reasonable, respectful, and related responses. (Gee, where have you heard that before? From *me*, remember?)

Alternative and Complimentary Therapies

If your child is feeling like stressed out or strung out, guilty, or depressed consider alternative therapies as well, perhaps a combination of family therapy *and* a weekly massage, or individual counseling *and* acupuncture. In times of stress, more than the mind needs to be nourished.

Getting Help for Yourself

Writer Alice Walker says that having a child is like having your heart walking around outside your body. When your heart is injured, you *feel* it. When your child is going through a hard time, you need support—a friend to cry on, a support group, a weekly therapy session (and of course a manicure and a massage). Invest in yourself.

Last Resorts

When nothing works (and I mean *nothing*) and your child is at risk of injuring himself or somebody else, you may need to take it a step further. I stress that these are last resorts, which is why I only give them a brief listing here.

- Intervention is a special meeting where people who love the child come forward to confront him about his problems, their concern, and the impact his problems are having on their lives. Intervention works best when it's held immediately after a crisis.

- Residential treatment is for patients who need round-the-clock care and/or observation. Residential treatment might be used for severe behavior problems, drug or alcohol addiction, mental illness, eating disorders, and so on. Residential treatment has a decent but not total success rate. It's a very drastic option.

- Calling in the law or having your child declared incorrigible are serious moves with possible lifelong ramifications. Consider long and hard before you take this final step; you risk losing your child forever.

Finally, remember life is long. The longer you live, the more apparent it is that the only permanent thing is change. Most traumas subside; most crises are resolved. The pain you and your child feel now will probably not last forever. People change, and situations clear up. If you can even for a moment stand back and stare at the stars or watch a baby learn to crawl, you'll regain your sense of hope. Never give up.

THE LEAST YOU NEED TO KNOW

- It's *always* hard to admit that your kid is having big trouble.

- Problems might be caused by undiagnosed ADD/ADHD.

- If your child is in trouble with the law, take 15 minutes to do *nothing*.

- Therapeutic training is important, but more important is the individual therapist and how you or your child "clicks" with her.

- You're doing the hiring. Interview the therapist, and shop around.

- "Alternative" therapies combine well with traditional therapy.

14

The Myth of the Terrible Mom!

Whoa, a whole chapter about guilt, failure, and feeling lousy? Not exactly. Look, teaching good discipline requires self-trust and self-respect, and momhood gets a bad rap in this society. It's hard to trust and respect yourself when all those nasty Negative Mom messages are drifting around like trash on a windy day. This mom thinks it's time for you to shovel some of that garbage off your lawn, to dispose of that pile of ugly debris labeled, "I'm a terrible mom."

As a mom, I want my kids to feel good about themselves, to stand up for themselves and for others. I respect them, and I want them to respect me back. If I'm not feeling good about my parenting, it's a sure shot *they* won't. Why will they listen to me about discipline, or about anything else?

THE NEGATIVE MOM MESSAGE

In our society, momhood is fraught with negativity and guilt. Since *Grimm's Fairy Tales* and before, moms have gotten the blame for everything. And nobody seems to like having their mom *around.* Take a look at that most American of traditions, the kid's movie. In almost every case, adventure begins when the kid is separated from the mom or the mom *dies.* Do you think I'm exaggerating? Here are just a few examples:

- *Bambi* (Mom dies)
- *Beauty and the Beast* (nonexistent Mom)
- *Cinderella* (dead Mom, evil Stepmom)
- *Dumbo* (Mom thrown in elephant prison)
- *The Hunchback of Notre Dame* (Mom dies)
- *The Little Mermaid* (nonexistent Mom)
- *The Secret Garden* (Mom dies, Dad dies, too)

You can continue the list, but my question remains: Geez, can't kids have any fun with their moms around?

Yes, you *can* have a good time with your kids! Keep in mind, though, that there's a lot of pressure in society for kids to think that moms are dumb, uncool, or meddling. (This is largely a societal thing. I'm mostly talking about Western cultures. In a number of other societies, kids don't rebel the same way.)

At certain stages in your kid's life, she's going to feel humiliated by your very existence. Your pleasures with her may need to become furtive ones: going out for dessert in a café that her friends would *never* go into or making holiday gifts in the privacy of your home. In private, Mom may not seem to be quite so dorky (and Junior might drop that *ridiculous* slouch).

THE SELF-RESPECTING MOM

Unfortunately, it's hard not to take society's (and your preadolescent kid's) Negative Mom messages to heart. Understanding the messages can help you understand more about how you feel about your own mothering.

Okay, be honest. You put up a good front, and everybody thinks, "Wow, she's really got it together." How do you feel inside? I've heard lots of moms say negative things about themselves and their parenting. Often they add, "Just joking," but are they?

Few people feel as good about themselves as they could. Since the culture's got this Negative Mom thing going on, it may never *tell* you what a good job you're doing. You're going to have to say it to yourself.

> **MOM ALWAYS SAID**
>
> Ah, motherhood—it's celebrated and cursed. Your challenge: To define what being a mom means for *you*. Don't let anybody (including yourself) throw that little word "*should*" your way.

You'll be most successful teaching discipline when you approach it with a positive stance. According to the Stanford Research Institute, success is 88 percent attitude. That's easily said, of course. Don't you hate it when people tell you, "Buck up! You need to work on your attitude"? If it were that easy, *everybody* would be successful at everything they do all the time!

There are lots of ways to improve your attitude, of course, and they aren't about "just bucking up." The best way is to take a look at your self-respect and see how it could be strengthened. Self-respect comes from self-appreciation, taking action, and getting positive feedback from the world. Now you can't count on the positive feedback from the world. But you *do* have control over your self-appreciation, and you can take action to improve yourself, to improve your family life, and to improve the world.

Self-acceptance and self-responsibility are vital to increasing self-respect. Look at yourself for who you are. Change the circumstances that you can change. And give yourself a break. (That's an order, soldier.)

HELP! I HATE MY KID, AND MY KID HATES ME!

But what if it's you? What if *you* don't want your kid around? What if you're *sick* of your kid? What does it mean when your kid seems to despise you? Does it mean you're a terrible mom? No, indeed. Take a look at what you're *really* feeling: anger, impatience, depression, and guilt.

Nobody said you have to like your kid all the time. Whoa, now *there's* a revolutionary thought, Mom! Think about it: Love isn't so easily killed. Remember your first true love affair? Don't you occasionally think about it and feel *love?* And that was years ago. My point is there is a difference between like and love. You *can* love the child and hate her actions. If your kid is being a jerk, you don't have to like her. She's not liking you, is she? (Temporary dislike may even be a natural stage in development, a part of separating.) Being a mom means unconditional love, not unconditional like. Really.

Rage, Anger, Losing It, and Fury

Let's talk about rage. It's one of the hidden issues in parenting. Moms put a lot of energy into being good mothers. They tend to think that a good mom is always calm and forgiving. Ridiculous! Everybody loses it occasionally.

No family member is immune to rage—parents or kids. A child's rage provides one of the *biggest* parenting challenges, in fact. Faced with a child's rage, your instinct may be to strike back, with your body or with your words. Whoa, Nellie! Count to 10! Conflict and anger are a normal part of life in a family, but rages can be disruptive and destructive, whether they're yours or your children's.

When you begin to understand the causes of your rage as well as methods of anger control and avoidance, you'll be better able to enjoy your child and your life as a mom. I recommend a book called *Taming the Dragon in Your Child: Solutions for Breaking the Cycle of Family Anger,* by Meg Eastman and Sydney Craft. It offers good tools for understanding and dealing with family conflict.

Impatience

Kids are designed to *push.* They push against their parents as they grow up, and they push their parents' emotional buttons. Face it, you're human, and there will be many times when they *will* get under your skin. Yes, it's vital to try to maintain patience, but it's normal to get impatient. It wouldn't be human to be calm and serene all the time. Impatience with children can occasionally lead to some pretty funny dialogue. "Oh, stop acting like a child!" "But I am a child, Mom." Here are a few patience tips:

◆ Pretend you're feeling patient even if you're not. The action of pretending can sometimes lead to the desired feeling. (You don't believe me? Try it.)

◆ Deep breathing can help. Deep breathing, unless it's in a carbon monoxide–filled room, can *always* help.

◆ Try to be more than *sympathetic;* try to *empathize* with your child and feel what she feels. Put yourself in her small (or not so small) garments; look at the world from her perspective. Remember being young? I'll bet you drove the grown-ups (and the little boys) crazy!

WISE WORDS

Sympathy means feeling for—but not necessarily under-standing—another person. *Empathy* means feeling what another person feels.

Depression

It's hard to be an effective mom when you're feeling sad or depressed. If you're very upset, your tolerance is reduced, your empathy tends to dry up, and your patience is gone. You don't really *hate* your child, you just don't have the emotional reserve to deal with her right now.

That's one reality. The other reality is that it isn't fair to your child if you remove yourself emotionally. You have a responsibility to take care of yourself so that you *can* take care of your child.

- ◆ Depression is often frustration that has been turned inward. Take some time off!

- ◆ Evaluate and reevaluate your life. What changes can you make?

- ◆ Go back and review my suggestions in Chapter 13 for finding some good therapy. Get out in nature, too. Take a walk in the woods. It may not help the overall picture, but it may help your tolerance level.

GUILT

Do you feel guilty about your parenting? Do you blame yourself for something that you did wrong? Most moms do. Guilt is both common and devastating. It certainly has a way of taking the joy out of life.

The lives of moms today are fraught with *issues,* and one of the biggies is about work. Guilt plays a big part here, too. Moms who stay home feel guilty. Moms who work outside the home feel guilty. Either way, moms lose. Look, nobody has the right answer; there may not be one. The important thing is knowing that everybody is simply doing the best they can.

Defeating Guilt

When you suffer from free-floating guilt, that sense that you're doing everything ever so slightly wrong, it's time for a little self-nurturing. Give yourself a break, and take a minivacation from guilt. Otherwise Guilty Mom may find herself morphing into Martyr Mom. Burn Martyr Mom at the stake and she'll feel guilty for polluting the atmosphere. Is that the model of a mother you want your children to grow up with? Hold it! I didn't mean you should feel guilty about it. Try some of the following tips. Remember, feeling guilty is a habit. It may take time to break it.

- ◆ Hire a baby-sitter, say, "I'm outta here," and go out to dinner with a friend or by yourself. While you're at it, have some guilt-free dessert.

- ◆ Hire a baby-sitter and go to a concert.

- ◆ Call up an old girlfriend or even an old boyfriend—*no*, not for romance!—and reminisce about the old days.

- ◆ Take an hour off from guilt. Set the timer. During that hour, refuse to feel guilty. Don't feel guilty about feeling guilty, and don't feel guilty for feeling guilty *about* feeling guilty. (And don't feel guilty about *not* feeling guilty either!)

MOM KNOWS BEST

Time flows only one way (kind of like gravity, unfortunately). You can't go back. Concentrate on doing better next time.

A Call to Action

Guilt doesn't have to be a totally negative force. At its best, guilt can be an alarm. Guilt is only effective when you listen to it. It says, "Hey, Mom, something's not right with this picture!" When you feel guilty about something (or about everything, as many moms do), step back. Look at the bigger picture.

Nobody is perfect, and many moms have things in their lives that they feel rightfully guilty about: something they could have done better or some time they truly blew it and did something that went against their values or beliefs. Guilt can incapacitate, and guilt can also teach. At its best (when you're really paying attention), guilt is a wake-up call—"Brinnnnnggg!! Good morning, Mom!"— calling you to face reality and begin making changes. Figuring out what you did that went against your convictions can teach you more about yourself. Healthy guilt can lead to more self-respect.

Misguided Guilt

Some people feel guilty over everything that goes wrong in their child's life. They feel guilty because they're not perfect, because they're not wealthy, and because they can't teach their child to speak Uzbekestani. Moms tend to feel guilty when they're not living up to an internal ideal of what a mom should be. Take a moment to think about it. Close your eyes and say the word "mom" to yourself. What comes to mind? Oops, are you trying to be Super Mom instead of Reasonable Mom again? That smiling, demonic Super Mom with her spotless house, fresh-baked lemon meringue pie, and career as a partner in a major law firm (on the side)? Cool it! You're fighting a ghost. Super Mom isn't any more real than the ugly monster in little Joannie's closet.

EVERYBODY MAKES MISTAKES

"The trouble with failure is that it feels like failure. That's never a nice feeling. What is generally not recognized is that's the only trouble with failure." (Jon Carroll, "On the Utility of Failure," *San Francisco Chronicle*, November 14, 1996.)

Failure, says Carroll, is just information, an "education with a hard-to-beat memory aid." He has a point. Painful as our failures and mistakes can be, they are how we learn.

In *Wonderful Ways to Love a Child*, Judy Ford cites a study in which two groups of students were taught spelling and math problems and then, after a break, given a test to see what they'd learned. When the students returned, they were taught more spelling and math. Again they were given a break, and, when they came back, they were retested on the same material. One of the two groups was scolded and told to "study harder" when they made mistakes; the other group was given gentle guidance and encouragement. The performance of the first group declined steadily, while that of the gentle guidance group improved. Bonus: The kids remembered *best* those words and problems they had missed and restudied.

And the Moral Is?

When mistakes happen, be gentle with yourself—and your kids, for that matter. Nobody is perfect. You're a human being; at least, I assume you are. You will say and do things you regret. You will neglect to say and do other things and then wish you had. Instead of letting your mistakes plunge you into a pit of slippery, slimy guilt, try using the mistake as a learning tool. That's what mistakes and failure are *for!*

Who Me, Apologize?

It's two little words: "I'm sorry." Have you noticed how some people spend their time saying them, while some refuse to say them at all?

The world is divided into two general types: those who like anchovies and those who do not. That's obvious. But have you noticed that you can also divide the world into people who say, "I'm sorry," at the drop of a hat and people who will never, ever— well, hardly ever—apologize?

These are separate groupings. Some "apologizers" like anchovies, some don't—there's no evidence of correlation. Here's the point I'm leading up to. If you have apologetic tendencies, be careful. There are certainly times when it's appropriate to apologize for your behavior and make restitution. But if you're feeling a little bit crummy about yourself, if you feel like a terrible mom, pay attention. Make sure you aren't becoming Apologetic Audrey, saying "I'm sorry" every time somebody *else* stubs their toes!

BEING REAL

Many moms, especially when they're wondering if they're terrible, think they should try to shelter their kids from the "awful truth," both about themselves and about the world. Some plaster a phony calm over a seething mass of human turmoil. Are these moms fooling anybody? No dice, sweetie. Be Real Mom. Kids have a built-in nonsense meter that tells them when something bogus is up. Lying or deceiving your kids casts an air of unreality over everything. What and who can they trust if not you?

Here's a horrific true-life story about a mom and dad who refused to be real. These two parents (I'll call them Connie and Bruce) had one child, a boy. They wanted to be good parents, as all parents do, and they were convinced that one way to do that was to keep their little boy from being exposed to the harsher side of life. And they did. They protected his mind from anything upsetting, even keeping him away from other children for fear that they might play with weapons or tease the child. Predictably, the child grew up anxious. What was this awful world that he couldn't even be told about? When he was four, a visiting friend from California mentioned earthquakes. "Shh!" Connie said, and Bruce waved frantically at the little boy. "He doesn't know about *those*." What happened? Well, of course, the boy grew, and in the course of things became more exposed to the world as it is. Because he hadn't been introduced to the sad, bad aspects of life with love, compassion, and understanding, he became more and more anxious, until at age eight he was institutionalized, unable to cope with the horrors of the world.

Being Real Mom is a big part of being Reasonable Mom. Real Mom is a real person. She doesn't put on an act in front of her kids, she doesn't pretend to be someone she isn't, and she's realistic about the world with her kids. In other words, she tells the truth. Kids need to learn that people make mistakes. They need to see you blowing it, reconsidering, changing your mind, apologizing or making amends, and doing better next time.

SO...YOU LAUGHED!

Are you afraid of encouraging your child's misbehavior by laughing? Part of being real is allowing humor to play a role in your parenting and your disciplining. One of Reasonable Mom's traits is that she sometimes laughs even when it seems inappropriate. And some of the anxiety of worrying about being Terrible Mom will evaporate if you just open your mouth, throw back your head, and *howl* like a hyena!

The Johnson family was eating in a restaurant, and the food was a long time coming. Ten-year-old Andrew was bored and hungry. He flicked a piece of ice from his water glass into the air. It spun over to the next table and landed inside another guest's water glass with a loud *kerplop*. The guest startled at the noise, looked around, looked under the table, couldn't locate where it had come from, shrugged, reached for his water glass, and took a big swallow. The whole thing took maybe five seconds. The Johnsons watched the entire series of events with mounting horror. Then, as the guest set the now-empty water glass down with a clunk and a loud "ahhh," they all—Mom, Dad, little sister, and Andrew—broke into hysterical laughter.

You're right, Andrew was acting out, and Mom and Dad should not have laughed. But hey, it was *funny!* Here's the thing: You can laugh *and* disapprove. Too often discipline is taught with a frown, as a *task*. No *wonder* people hate the idea of discipline. It seems so *unpleasant*.

When you find yourself forgetting to laugh with life, remind yourself:

◆ Laughter says "I love you," and "I love you" is always a good place to begin teaching discipline.

◆ Laughter is physically healthy for your body. It promotes healing in times of injury or illness.

◆ Don't be afraid of occasionally laughing at times you "shouldn't." It's part of being real.

There are times, of course, when humor is inappropriate: when it hurts feelings, when it sends the wrong message (when the behavior is *too* inappropriate or actually harmful), when a child feels very vulnerable, or when humor is used instead of communication.

Open communication is *hard*. In some families, members use laughter and humor as a survival mechanism. In others, humorous banter is the primary means of communication. Humor has its place. It's not meant to substitute for the heartfelt talking—and listening—that children need.

THE POWER OF CHANGE

They say personal change requires, first of all, a desire to change. I believe it. It's also true that the only thing you can truly rely on in life *is* change. Life is in flux, and many things in your life will change without your effort. When you're feeling stuck in life, it's hard to believe that things—and you—will ever be different. Well, they will be. Some things change without your effort, and some things require hard work, hard work, hard work…and a leap of faith.

Change takes time. Say you read this book and decide to change your approach to teaching discipline. Then you find yourself making the same old mistakes again and again. Chin up, Mom: You can *still* change. Change takes time. Stay the course!

"You must be the change you wish to see in the world," said Mahatma Ghandi.

THE LEAST YOU NEED TO KNOW

◆ Self-acceptance and self-responsibility are vital to increasing self-respect.

◆ It's unconditional love, not unconditional like. Nobody said you have to like your kid all the time.

◆ Feelings of rage, impatience, depression, and guilt are common and normal.

◆ Mistakes and failure are important tools for learning.

◆ You're a real person—act like it! Lies and phony faces won't wash.

◆ When in doubt, try laughter.

◆ Change takes time. Keep at it.

15

Respecting Each Other

Wow! It's the last chapter in the book! This is where, when they're making a movie in Hollywood, the director shouts, "Pull focus!" and the camera sweeps back to see the larger picture, the *context* in which the love scene or reconciliation is happening. In this chapter, I pull focus and take a final look at *family*. Good discipline happens within the context of families, whatever their shape or size.

THE RESPECTFUL FAMILY—A PORTRAIT

I know, you're sitting in your living room. Chaos reigns. You've got a screaming mess of sloppy kids careening through the house. Everybody's doing things too fast, and nothing's getting done. Step back. Close your eyes. What do you *feel?* Tension, distrust, and anxiety? Or warmth, love, and connection? Maybe some of each?

Some strange ideas about family are floating around out there. "I can show them my worst and they'll still love me." Have you ever said that? Or, "Where else can I let down my hair and be myself (translation: *rude*)?" Remember the story of the man who courted his wife with candlelit dinners and chivalrous behavior and then, on their honeymoon, said (as he scratched himself, belched, and clicked on the TV), "I'm so glad we're married. Now we can stop being so NICE to each other."

Attention, campers! This is your *family* you're talking about—the ones most precious to you in all the world. Show them a little *respect*, will ya?

A respectful family isn't about family configuration, and it's not about specific patterns of behavior. A respectful family is a group of people who care about each other, who are *there* for each other, who listen to each other, who usually live with each other, and who are doing the best they can.

To be sure, this is a loose definition. Mom says, "It's the love that matters, not the shape of that love."

RAISING AN ADULT YOU'D WANT TO KNOW

When your child was an infant, time seemed to last forever. As writer Alisa Kwitney says in her essay "The Eternal Now" (from *Child of Mine,* a collection of essays edited by Christina Baker Kline), "It is hard to get perspective in the constant rush of teething biscuit, scum on hair, unwashed dishes, and desperate reachings for dangerous objects." Remember? Back then, it was impossible to imagine a time when Baby wouldn't be a month old and sleeping only two hours at a stretch.

As your kid grew, so did your perspective. A bit. It's always hard to imagine the future. It's *hard* to keep a sense of perspective about it all. Not to pull rank on you younger moms, but the younger you are, the harder it is. Remember that mom who had the baby at age 63? No, I'm not getting involved in *that* debate. But I will say I bet she has a *great* sense of perspective.

Look at your child. She's growing, and soon she'll be grown and gone. Who do you see her becoming? How do you raise her to be an adult that you would like to know even if she weren't your child?

The Traits Exercise

I believe that, in order to achieve a goal, you had first better define what that goal is. This exercise helps you *think* about your disciplinary and parenting goals. It asks the question, "Who would you like your child to be?" Then it turns the question around: "Who would *you* like to be?"

In this exercise you will choose from a list of positive traits. It may be hard to choose—*all* the traits are positive. This exercise is about prioritizing, and prioritizing is *always* hard.

1. From the following list, choose the top three traits you want your kid to have as an adult. Write them in spaces 1, 2, and 3 in the left-hand column of the following table (you can abbreviate).

TOP THREE TRAITS	*SECOND THREE TRAITS*	*THIRD THREE TRAITS*
1. _____	4. _____	7. _____
2. _____	5. _____	8. _____
3. _____	6. _____	9. _____

2. Choose three more traits—the next three traits you would like your child to have when she's grown. Write them in spaces 4, 5, and 6 (the middle column). Then choose three more—write them in spaces 7, 8, and 9.

3. Check in with yourself. Are you surprised by the traits you chose? Are there traits I didn't include on the list that you want to? Do you want to change anything on the list? Go ahead.

4. Now, do the same exercise again, prioritizing the top nine traits you would like to describe *you.*

TOP THREE TRAITS	*SECOND THREE TRAITS*	*THIRD THREE TRAITS*
1. _____	4. _____	7. _____
2. _____	5. _____	8. _____
3. _____	6. _____	9. _____

The List

Financial acuity (ability to prosper)
Entrepreneurial spirit (energy, ambition)
Lasting contributor to human knowledge
Ability to mediate, to make peace
Artistic sensibility and ability
Ability to fit in
Sense of fairness
Happiness
Sense of responsibility to family
Kindness and charity
Independent thinker
Independent

Complacency (sense of comfort)
Honesty
Inner harmony and serenity
Rich inner life
Ability to form mature friendships
Ability to form mature sexual relationships
Loyalty to family and friends
Loyalty to employer
Loyalty to nation
Agent of social change
Savvy (not easy to fool)
Scholarly aptitude (good student)
Loving
Lovable
Ability to relish pleasure
Spirituality or religious spirit
Self-respect and self-esteem
Respect and admiration for others
Wisdom (mature understanding of life)

Questions About the Exercise

Now that you've completed filling out the tables, here are some questions to think about:

◆ How do the two completed tables compare?

◆ Many people find that the traits they've chosen for their child closely mirror the traits they've chosen for themselves. Do the traits you've chosen for your child match her abilities, interests, and temperament?

◆ How do the traits you've chosen for yourself differ from the traits you've chosen for your child?

◆ Was there anything about this exercise that surprised you?

◆ Look at the traits you've chosen for your child. Is your approach to teaching discipline likely to encourage those traits?

◆ What can you change in your approach to teaching discipline to move your child—or yourself—closer to your goals?

Trust your child's choices. Don't force your own thoughts, dreams, and ambitions on him. He has his own life, thought process, and personality. Model your values...then step back.

It's a Troublesome Trait—Now

It's odd but true: The character and temperamental traits that most irritate or infuriate you now may be the same traits that will make your child the wonderful, strong adult you would like him to be.

Rayna was not an easy child by any stretch. From the time she was very small, she knew what she wanted, she had an implacable sense of justice ("That's not *fair!!!*"), and she didn't put up with anybody standing in her way—adult or child. At the beginning of her fifth-grade year, her fourth-grade teacher grabbed her new teacher in the hallway. "I see you've got Rayna Metry in your class this year. Just remember, when we're old and gray, Rayna will be out fighting for our rights."

There's an old saying, "Little pitchers have big ears." Even if you *think* your child is out of earshot when you talk about her, you're probably wrong. She knows what you think—and say—about her. Listen to yourself talk. "Angel's been impossible these days. She's such a demanding kid." Angel—who is no devil—overhears you. She thinks, "I'm impossible. I'm demanding," and (because this is how human beings work) she believes it, she internalizes it, and she works harder at becoming *more* impossible and *more* demanding. Why don't you try to change your terminology?

All people have areas of "challenge" in their personalities, and your kid is certainly not the exception.

In a Positive Light...

This exercise was inspired by the work of Mary Sheedy Kurcinka, author of the book, *Raising Your Spirited Child*. In the blank spaces in the left column, list some of your child's negative character traits. In the right column, "recast" those traits in a more positive light. I've started for you.

NEGATIVE TRAIT	POSITIVE RECASTING
Stubborn and bull-headed	Assertive and persistent
Impulsive	Spontaneous and flexible
Anxious	Cautious
Shy	Reserved and soft-spoken
Wild	Energetic
Slow	Thoughtful and deliberate
Spacy	Creative
_____	_____
_____	_____
_____	_____
_____	_____
_____	_____

CELEBRATING THE FAMILY

A strong family identity is a foundation for your child to stand on. A strong family provides a child with a set of allies in life. You can build a strong family identity if there are two of you or twenty of you. Numbers and configurations don't matter.

The family rules and family values exercises in Chapter 4 can help your family gain a stronger identity. The suggestions below can help as well.

MOM KNOWS BEST

When you celebrate your family, you say to each other, "We're glad to be a family. We're glad that we love each other."

Celebrate Your Heritage

Where does your family come from? Are your roots Jewish, African-American, Irish, Malaysian, Cuban, Greek, Chinese, Nigerian, or Bengali? Part of what makes your family special is a shared sense of history and culture. Strengthening a sense of culture gives your children a sense of history, continuity, and future. Here are some thoughts and tips on ways to enhance your child's sense of her historical and cultural roots:

◆ Language is an important aspect of culture. When the "old" language is lost, part of the culture is lost as well.

◆ Talk with your child about your culture's customs, whether or not you practice them today.

◆ Cultural dances, music, and dress may seem dorky to your children now, but they'll appreciate these things later. If they resist your efforts, try introducing them in small doses. *Don't* surprise your child by performing a traditional dance on the table at the pizza parlor during her birthday party.

The Family Foods

Whether it's Tibetan momos, jello molds, white bread and mayonnaise sandwiches, oxtail stew, or spanakopita, family foods are an important part of a family's identity. Family foods need not come from your original heritage: Bill's chicken curry with house-ground spices is famous among his Jewish family and friends. Wei-Chu, who grew up in Singapore, makes a killer lasagna that her kids think of when they want some "comfort food."

I know, life is rushed; you don't have time to cook the way Grandma did. It's not your lifestyle. Cooking every day sounds a little too back-to-the-land for your taste, or maybe it sounds nice but just isn't feasible. But what about Aunt Reeva's blintzes or Grandma Annie's fudge? What about Cousin Tilly's pecan pie made with Southern Comfort? (Oops, I told the secret ingredient!) If your kids never taste these delicacies, they'll never know that these are the family foods. Here are some suggestions for incorporating family foods into your kids' lives:

- Try for once a month at first. Then maybe twice a month.

- Let the kids know that these meals are mandatory. If they squawk, say, "Look, sharing these foods is very important to me. This is part of your heritage. You can choose whether or not to like them." (After they taste the obligatory taste, you can break out the macaroni and cheese.)

- You say you're a lousy cook? Many cookbooks are suitable for children. Try learning together. (Even if it doesn't help *your* cooking, it may help your child's. You'll all reap the benefits!)

- Boys need to learn to cook, too (just a little reminder...).

The Family Mythology

A great way to build a strong sense of family identity is to share your cultural and personal stories. Children love birth stories, disaster stories, the tale of Mom's brush with pneumonia in France, the time Uncle Ray jumped into the lake, how Mommy and Daddy met, how Great-Grandpa Abe escaped from Russia, and how Grandma spanked the girls when they got into her lipstick. Here are some important things to remember about family stories:

- Stories build family and cultural identity. When Anaya runs into Cousin Alexandra in 20 years, they'll both know about the time that Grandma Karla roller-skated down the steepest hill in San Francisco. They'll both be able to sing all the words from "A Russian Lullaby."

- ◆ Stories teach values and consequences, and they do it in a casual, non-moralistic way.

- ◆ Stories help your kids see you as a person. If Tony comes home from school feeling lousy because somebody teased him about his acne, you can tell him about the time your face was so broken out that nobody would invite you to the eighth-grade dance. Knowing you've been there can help him through a hard time.

- ◆ Family stories teach children what life is like in their little corner of the world and how life differs from where the family originally came from.

- ◆ Your stories, cultural and personal, are a part of your children's history. They deserve to know the truth.

MOM KNOWS BEST

Kids love the "What were you like as a kid" game. Junior picks an age (say, 11), and you tell a true life story from that time. They'll love the "naughty" ones!

A family is built through shared experiences—in the rough times as well as the smooth. Model the value of family. Stand up for family members. Put up third cousins for a night when they pass through town (and make them tell stories about Great Uncle Angelo).

NURTURING CREATIVITY

Creativity enhances discipline; discipline enhances creativity. The more discipline in your life, the better, and by now you know that I don't mean military marching. Discipline and artistic expression are ways of focusing the mind. They both provide paths for learning.

In *interdisciplinary art*, the artist thinks about what she wants to say or explore in the artwork. Then she chooses the medium (or media) to satisfy those goals. For example, an interdisciplinary artist working on the travel theme might work with film, watercolors, folk dances, and epic poetry.

It's the same with parenting. As a mom, you'll use a variety of media—nurturing, encouragement, limits, consequences, and so on—to achieve your goals.

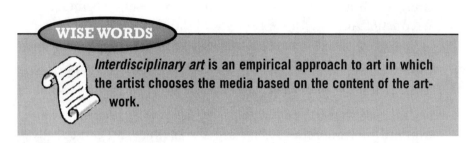

WISE WORDS

Interdisciplinary art is an empirical approach to art in which the artist chooses the media based on the content of the artwork.

Creativity as Fall-Back

Life does not always go well. Some wise soul once said, "Life is just about as hard as it can be, and no harder." There are times when *all* people are pushed to the edge of despair or grief, when everything in life seems to be collapsing. In times like this, art can nourish the soul as few other things can. A creative hobby, whether carving totem poles, painting murals, playing piccolo, or dancing hip hop, can replenish your energies. You don't have to be good at it; you don't even have to consider yourself "creative" (most people don't). The mere *action* of making, doing, or dancing can ease the soul. If you introduce your child to a range of artistic expressions now, he'll be more likely to have an outlet—an artistic fall-back, as it were—when he gets older.

Raising a Creative Child

Creativity comes in many forms. Here are some ideas to get you started:

◆ *Bring artistic expression into your child's life.* Paint or do hobbies with him, and always be *positive.* Don't overcorrect or judge.

◆ *Art should not be goal-oriented.* Try playing with clay, and try *not* keeping the results. It's very freeing to smush that clay back into mush when you're done.

◆ *Encourage fantasy.* Turn off the TV. Read to your child. Have your child read to you.

◆ *Music classes are available in most communities,* and they're not necessarily expensive. You don't need to pony up for a grand piano plus pricey piano lessons from the local Julliard graduate (well, not until your child is beg, beg, begging for more than two hours a day practice time...). How about guitar? (Acoustic! Acoustic! Don't kill me, I didn't say electric!)

◆ *Don't nag your child about practicing.* If your child has a hard time with self-motivation, try a class where there's no practice time or homework. Keep the experience positive.

◆ *Not all "art" forms are for all kids.* Try a few. She may be a natural on the trapeze and *hate* basket weaving. You can't really lose: The more exposure a child has to creative work or play, the better.

Encourage creative activities in your child's life and, in a while, you'll have the benefit of being able to say, when Willy gets whiny, "Why don't you go play your violin?"

MOM KNOWS BEST

Feeling uncreative? Feeling stuck? A number of good books on creative process can help, including Julia Cameron's wonderful workbook, *The Artist's Way.*

UP CLOSE AND PERSONAL

The respectful family is not respectful from a distance. Your child needs physical affection (so do you). He needs companionship, and he needs to see you unwound, relaxed, and kicking back in enjoyment. Hug, hug, and hug again. Physical affection is appropriate and needed. Play some games, and hug a little more. Yell, "You're fantastic," as your kid races out the door.

No matter what age she is, every child has her joys, and so does her family. It's so hard to remember that sometimes! When you're in the middle of family conflict, when you're as frustrated as a fly on the window pane, take a step back. Pay attention to the larger picture. Look for the joys.

Raising a respectful family is hard work. Give yourself credit for the effort, and celebrate your successes.

MOM ALWAYS SAID

Got an extra hour? Forget the messy house, crumbs, and dust bunnies. Spend time with your family, and have fun. Don't get hung up in surface appearances. Go for the real.

Suggestions for Special Time and Family Outings

Discipline is best taught by a parent who truly *knows* her child—her interests and reactions—and knowledge is based on shared experience. Shared experience is also the basis for strong family ties. Spend time together. Here's a beginner list of suggestions. Why don't you spend some time during your next family meeting generating others?

- Sign up for music camp together.

- Ferry rides. Train rides. Horseback rides.

- Take a bike ride together. (Wow! Fun *and* exercise!)

- Make your kid teach you how to skateboard. (Wear those knee pads. You don't need to share the experience of arthroscopic surgery.)

- Sign up for a family cruise. (Make sure it's not a seniors or singles party afloat.)

- Evening picnics. (Grab a blanket and some sandwiches and head for the park.)

- Meet for a late lunch near your office and take off work for the rest of the day. An older child can take public transportation to meet you there, and you can go home together.

- Art museums often have special exhibits for kids and families.

- Zoos! Zoos! Zoos!

- Many cities have natural history museums—fun for all, boring for none (and you'll get an education, too).

- Sports events. A baseball game gives a family a lot of hang-out time and a good opportunity for *bonding.*

- Nature-based activities: hiking, swimming, sailing, fishing, camping, canoeing, and diving. Feel family tensions magically dissipate, and see misbehavior disappear—poof!—into thin, clear, natural air.

THE PROCESS OF DISCIPLINE

Here's a final question for you (pop quiz!): What do Eastern studies, martial arts, gardening, fly fishing, the creative arts, and disciplining your children have in common?

Answer: All focus as much on the *process* as the result.

Raising your children is a big chunk of your life, physical and emotional. Life is not like a math test; there's no quantifiable way to score it. As you move through the process of parenthood, remember that childhood, too, is a process, and discipline is part of it. Teaching your children the process of discipline is an essential part of your daily life as a mom. Enjoy it.

THE LEAST YOU NEED TO KNOW

- Respectful families come in all shapes and sizes.

- Your child's "difficult" personality traits may become part of her strengths and individuality as an adult.

- Creativity can enhance discipline and provide fall-back emotional nourishment.

- Affection, attention, and shared time are vital to family health.

- Keep your eyes on the larger picture, and never give up.

- Enjoy the process.

Glossary

Active listening A communication technique where one party speaks and then the other party paraphrases what has been said.

Ally Somebody you can count on—whenever and however. An ally might be a friend, a relative, or a stranger. Allies can be more important than friends.

Anorexia An eating disorder characterized by self-starvation.

Attention Deficit Disorder A biochemical disorder in the orbital-frontal cortex of the brain, causing inattention, impulsiveness, hyperactivity, and distractibility.

Bribe Something promised in advance to try and bring about positive behavior.

Bulimia An eating disorder characterized by cycles of bingeing (overeating) and self-induced purging (vomiting and/or overuse of laxatives).

Compromise A conflict resolution technique where both parties give up a little of what they want in order to come to an agreement.

Consequences What happens as a result of a behavior, good or bad.

Consistency Sameness. The same rules and results over time.

Constructive criticism A form of critique in which the critic plays an instructional role. As education *cannot* occur in a hostile climate, constructive criticism *must* be done in a supportive and gentle manner.

Cooperation Working together to achieve a mutual goal.

Corporal punishment "Punishing the body." It's corporal punishment whether you hit your child softly or hard, with your hand or a belt, one time or ten times, frequently or once in a while.

Descriptive praise   A form of encouragement that describes what you like about a child's actions. It uses specific commentary rather than generalities.

Disapproval   A disciplinary tactic using clear, calm language to let a child know of your disappointment and anger at his or her behavior.

Discipline   The process of instilling values in your child through example, encouragement, and gentle guidance. Discipline comes from the word "disciple," meaning "a pupil," and the dictionary definition of discipline includes words like "instruction," "teaching," "learning," and "to train or develop."

Empathy   Feeling what another person feels.

Encouragement   A form of positive reinforcement that focuses on a child's efforts—rather than results—and helps a child become self-motivated.

Family   A grouping of people—usually but not always biologically or legally related—who may live together and who love and rely on each other.

Family meeting   A regularly scheduled, focused way to pay attention to the inner workings of *your* family unit and to help build inner discipline—structure—into your family life.

Family rules   The bottom-line behavior expectations of your particular family. Examples: "Our family does not use violence to settle problems." Or, "We do not eat meat in this house." Family rules are based on your family's deep-seated values.

Family time   Fun time spent together as an entire family.

Grounding   A form of removing privileges. The child loses her freedom for a short period of time.

"I" statement   A statement about your perceptions, feelings, or preferences prefaced with the word "I." "I" statements let the listener know that you're speaking from your own point of view.

Ignoring   A disciplinary tactic in which behavior is actively "ignored." When you want to avoid drawing attention to a misbehavior, try actively ignoring it.

Interdisciplinary art   An empirical approach to art. The artist chooses the media based on the content of the artwork.

Latency   The mid-childhood period between the ages of 7 and 11 when sexual interest seems to wane.

Limits Behavior boundaries. Some are set by nature (you can't fly), some are set by the state (you can't drive 100 mph), and some are set by you. It's up to you to define what your family considers acceptable or unacceptable behavior.

Parent blindness A syndrome suffered by parents who, because they love their kids, want the best for them, and don't want to believe things aren't going well for them, cannot see what's truly going on in their kids' lives. As the saying goes, *denial is not a river in Egypt.*

Parent deafness An unfortunate syndrome that makes kids with otherwise perfect hearing completely deaf to the wishes or needs of a parental figure.

Parenting partner Anybody with whom you share parenting or child care on a full- or part-time basis. It includes any adults who have direct involvement with or influence on your child's life.

Positive discipline An approach to discipline that incorporates encouragement, praise, trust, and respect for children through firm, wise limits. It teaches children to make their own choices and to understand the consequences of their choices. When necessary, it provides related, respectful, and reasonable responses to misbehavior.

Positive intent The underlying positive meaning behind any action.

Positive reinforcement Supporting your child's positive deeds and qualities through enthusiasm, encouragement, specific praise, and rewards. It reinforces what the child is doing right, rather than focusing on what the child is doing wrong.

Proactive listening A "guided" listening technique designed to elicit specific information.

Problem solving Using talking and listening techniques to collaborate so that both "sides" are happy.

Reward Something nice offered in response to positive behavior.

Safer sex Sexual activity with reduced risk of STDs—using condoms, dams, and activities that don't share body fluids.

Sexual misbehavior Misbehavior that has a sexual aspect. It should be handled like other misbehaviors—look for the positive intent, figure out the needs, and apply appropriate consequences.

Special time   Time spent alone in duos—one parent and one child. Special time is supposed to be *fun*. No chores allowed.

Sympathy   Feeling for—but not necessarily understanding—another person.

Temperament   The way a person approaches the world. It includes things such as energy level, regularity, first reaction, adaptability, intensity, mood, persistence, perceptiveness, and sensitivity.

Time-out (thinking time)   A disciplinary approach that removes the child from the situation in which she's having a hard time acting appropriately.

Resources

American Academy of Pediatrics. *Caring for Your School-Age Child: Ages 5 to 12.* New York: Bantam Books, 1995.

Ames, Louise Bates, Ph.D., et al. *Your Ten-to-Fourteen-Year-Old.* New York: Delacorte Press, 1988.

Baker Kline, Christina (editor). *Child of Mine: Writers Talk About the First Year of Motherhood.* New York: Hyperion Books, 1997.

Colin, Ann. *Willie: Raising and Loving a Child with Attention Deficit Disorder.* New York: Viking, 1997.

Eastman, Meg, Ph.D., and Sydney Craft Rosen. *Taming the Dragon in Your Child: Solutions for Breaking the Cycle of Family Anger.* New York: John Wiley and Sons, 1994.

Elium, Don and Jeanne. *Raising a Son: Parents and the Making of a Healthy Man.* Berkeley: Celestial Arts, 1994, 1996.

Elium, Jeanne and Don Elium. *Raising a Daughter: Parents and the Awakening of a Healthy Woman.* Berkeley: Celestial Arts, 1994.

Elium, Jeanne and Don Elium. *Raising a Family: Living on Planet Parenthood.* Berkeley: Celestial Arts, 1997.

Ford, Judy. *Wonderful Ways to Love a Child.* Berkeley: Conari Press, 1995.

Goldstein, Robin with Janet Gallant. *Stop Treating Me Like a Kid: Everyday Parenting: the 10- to 13-year-old.* New York: Penguin Books, 1994.

Joslin, Karen Renshaw. *Positive Parenting from A to Z.* New York: Fawcett Columbine, 1994.

Kurcinka, Mary Sheedy. *Raising Your Spirited Child.* New York: Harper Perennial, 1992.

Kutner, Lawrence, Ph.D. *Your School-Age Child.* New York: William Morrow and Co., 1996.

Lerman, Saf. *Parent Awareness Training: Positive Parenting for the 1980s.* New York: A and W Publishers, 1980.

Maag, John W., Ph.D. *Parenting Without Punishment: Making Problem Behavior Work for You.* Philadelphia: The Charles Press, 1996.

Mitchell, Grace and Lois Dewsnap. *Common Sense Discipline: Building Self-Esteem in Young Children: Stories from Life.* Glen Burnie: Telshare Publishing Company, 1995.

Riera, Michael. *Uncommon Sense for Parents with Teenagers.* Berkeley: Celestial Arts, 1995.

Rubin, Nancy. *Ask Me If I Care: Voices from an American High School.* Berkeley: Ten Speed Press, 1994.

Schwebel, Robert, Ph.D. *Saying No Is Not Enough: Raising Children Who Make Wise Decisions About Drugs and Alcohol.* New York: Newmarket Press, 1989.

Sonnenschein, William. *The Practical Executive and Workforce Diversity.* Chicago: NTC Publishing Group, 1997.

Villani, Sue Lanci with Jane E. Ryan. *Motherhood at the Crossroads: Meeting the Challenge of a Changing Role.* New York: Insight Books, 1997.

Windell, James. *8 Weeks to a Well-Behaved Child.* New York: Macmillan, 1994.

Windell, James. *Discipline, A Sourcebook of 50 Failsafe Techniques for Parents.* New York: Collier Books, 1991.

Index